D0515185

Dutch Soccer Drills

Volume 2: Game Action Drills

Richard Kentwell

MASTERS PRESS

A Division of Howard W. Sams & Co.

Published by Masters Press
A Division of Howard W. Sams & Company
2647 Waterfront Pkwy E. Dr, Suite 100, Indianapolis, IN 46214

96 97 98 99 00 01   10 9 8 7 6 5 4 3 2 1

Library of Congress Cataloging-in-Publication Data Pending

Contents

Acknowledgments

I should like to thank Henny Kormelink and Egbert van Hes for allowing me to bring their "De Kartotheek" to North America and Roger Bongaerts, Director of The Dutch Soccer Academy, for his many hours translating and facilitating the drills.

Cover photography courtesy of Empics Sports Photo Agency. Matthew Ashton, Photographer.

Cover Design by Phil Velikan.

INTRODUCTION

Dutch Soccer Drills is an aid to creating carefully balanced coaching sessions. The various small sided games and drills are indexed by subject to make it easy to find the drills you need. The value of *Dutch Soccer Drills* is instantly recognizable. How many times has the following scenario happened to you?

Tonight I have another coaching session. I have no idea which drills I will use. After the last match, the team's shortcomings were fairly obvious. Although we won, we missed far too many goal-scoring opportunities early in the match. We lost the ball too often in midfield, and if the opposition had been sharper we would have conceded a few goals. Something was definitely wrong. Maybe I need to vary the coaching drills I have been using recently. Introduce more obstacles. Gear the exercises more closely to the match situations. Differentiate more. Which player are lacking in self-confidence? Which players still have conditional shortcomings? What should I concentrate on specifically in the coming weeks in the context of our scheduled opponents? And on top of all of that, I need drills which can motivate and capture my players' imagination.

Lots of questions for which there are lots of possible answers.

While the match itself offers endless opportunities for creating coaching drills, it is still imperative to have a book containing match-related, small sided games and coaching drills. When planning a coaching program it is important to select the most appropriate drills. *Dutch Soccer Drills* is an excellent aid for devising such a program. A match analysis should be carried out beforehand. This soccer book is an ideal tool to use in conjunction with an in-depth match analysis.

A coach sees a great deal during a match. We usually look first to see whether players are carrying out the tasks they have been assigned. Obviously we are also interested in the result. The impressions gathered during a match are lost after a few hours and certainly after a few days have passed. We can then no longer recall the consecutive phases of the game. If we won, everything must have gone well. If we lost, we look for the moments in the game which were crucial to losing it. In both cases we are taking a one-sided approach to the match. It would be better to make notes on the positive and negative aspects of each match, with a view to remembering strengths and improving weaknesses. This point of departure is always the player. His technical development and tactical insight determine which drills are best for him. Each page shows a diagram with the correct sequence of move. It also shows the objective of the drills, guidelines relating to the organization, instructions which can be given during the drill, and a number of possible variations. When a coach devises a coaching program, it is essential that enough attention is paid to each type of drill. The focus should not be on the result of the next match but on developing players with good technical skills and tactical insight, and the ability to solve the problems with which they are confronted during games of soccer.

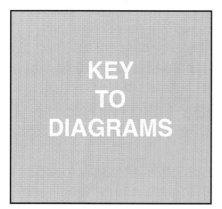

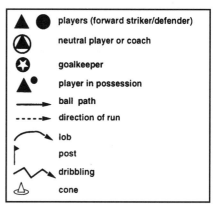

	players (forward striker/defender)
	neutral player or coach
	goalkeeper
	player in possession
	ball path
	direction of run
	lob
	post
	dribbling
	cone

STEPS FOR USING DUTCH SOCCER DRILLS

1. Analysis

• What are the strong and weak points of the team?

• Which phase of training are we in?

• How have we tried to improve weak points until now?

2. Objective — choice of subject

• What can we achieve in a single coaching session?

• Which subject is important in the context of developments to date or with regard to the next opponent?

3. Planning the coaching session

• Which methodical aspects should be taken into account?

• How should I dose the workload?

• Which small sided games and practice drills should I choose?

4. Giving the coaching session

• Should specific exercises be carried out longer or more intensively?

• Has the desired effect been achieved?

• Do the corrections and instructions bring the desired results?

5. Evaluations of the coaching session

• Did everything go to plan?

• Were the players motivated?

• Did the players learn anything?

Chapter 1

COMBINATION PLAYS

COMBINATION PLAY   1

OBJECTIVE:	Improving combination play
NUMBER OF PLAYERS:	2 (pairs)
TIME:	5 minutes per station
EQUIPMENT:	1 ball per 2 players

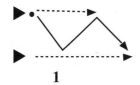

1

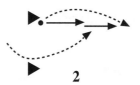

2

3

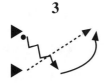

4

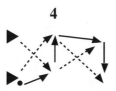

ORGANIZATION:	Players use different passes to practice combinations. 1. Diagonal pass into run of partner. 2. Forward pass into run, overlap. 3. Dribble, player 2 makes diagonal run, pass into run. 4. Short pass forward or square, diagonal run by player receiving ball.
INSTRUCTIONS:	Let players work on combinations for 5 minutes before switching to next combination play.
COACHING POINTS:	• Accurate passing (correct direction and pace). • Eye contact between players. • Pass into the run. • Player without ball must ask for ball.
VARIATIONS:	Use defenders.

COMBINATION PLAY

OBJECTIVE: Improving 1-2 combination

NUMBER OF PLAYERS: Groups of 4

AREA/FIELD: 20 yards x 30 yards

TIME: 10-15 minutes

EQUIPMENT: 1 ball per 4 players

1-2 combination

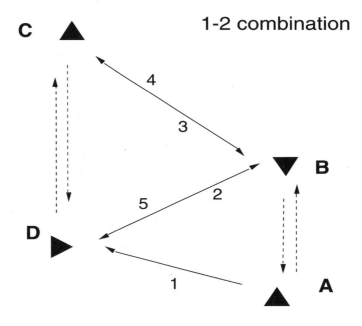

ORGANIZATION: Player A passes to player D, D passes to B. Player B passes to C and changes position with player A. Player C passes back to A and changes position with player D.

INSTRUCTIONS: Start off using 2 touches.

COACHING POINTS:
- Accurate passing.
- Quick change off position.
- Play ball to correct foot with correct pace.

VARIATIONS: Play everything 1 touch.

COMBINATION PLAY   **3**

OBJECTIVE:	Improving combination play, runs on and off ball
NUMBER OF PLAYERS:	9-16 players
AREA/FIELD:	30 yard x 30 yard grid
TIME:	15 minutes
EQUIPMENT:	4 cones, supply of balls

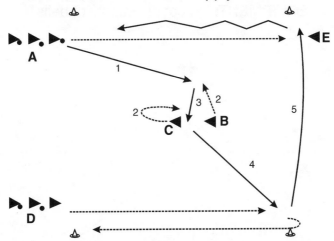

ORGANIZATION:
- Player A passes ball to player B in middle of grid.
- Player B plays ball to player C after player C made initial movement away from ball. Player C plays ball into run of player D (Run to cone). Player D plays cross pass to player E.
- Player E dribbles ball back to starting position.

INSTRUCTIONS: Start with 2 touch and work toward 1 touch/game speed.

COACHING POINTS:
- Eye contact and communication.
- Pass ball to correct foot.
- Pass ball at right time, into run of moving players.

COMBINATION PLAY 4

OBJECTIVE: • Improving 1 touch play
• Improving long combination and linking up

NUMBER OF PLAYERS: 12-16 players

AREA: 40 yards x 30 yards

TIME: 15 minutes

EQUIPMENT: 6 cones, supply of balls

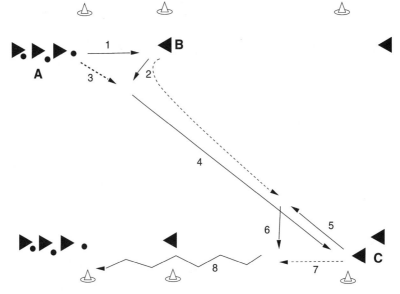

ORGANIZATION: Player A and B play 1-2 combination. Player A passes long to player C (diagonal). Player B follows long pass to link up with player C. Player B and C play 1-2 combination. Player C collects ball and dribbles to opposite end of grid. Drill starts over again.

COACHING POINTS: • Quick, accurate passing.
• Pass to correct foot.
• Quick run to link up.

VARIATIONS: Introduce defenders.

COMBINATION PLAY   5

OBJECTIVE:	Improving long 1-2 combination
NUMBER OF PLAYERS:	6-8
AREA/FIELD:	20 yards x 25 yards
TIME:	15 minutes
EQUIPMENT:	4 cones, supply of balls

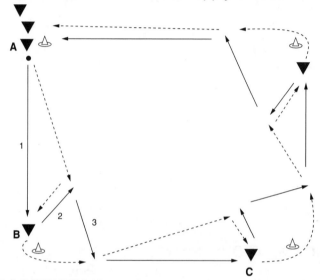

ORGANIZATION:
- Player A passes long to player B. Player B lays off ball to player A who made run following pass. After pass, Player B sprints around cone and receives ball into run by player A.
- Player B repeats drill with player C.

INSTRUCTIONS:
- Carry out drill with 2 balls. Start with player A and C at same time.
- Go clockwise and counter clockwise.

COACHING POINTS:
- Quick movement after pass (smart movement).
- Communication and eye contact.
- Accurate passing.
- Play 1 touch.

COMBINATION PLAY 6

OBJECTIVE:	Improving long combination play and movement off ball
NUMBER OF PLAYERS:	6-12 players
AREA/FIELD:	20 yards x 25 yards
TIME:	15 minutes
EQUIPMENT:	4 cones, supply of balls

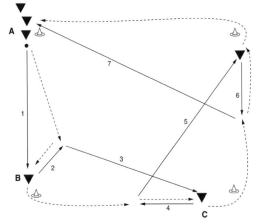

ORGANIZATION:	Player A plays long ball to player B and follows pass. Player B plays short combination back to player A and sprints around cone. Player A plays ball to player C. Player C plays ball into run of player B and sprints around cone. Player B plays long ball to player D. Player D plays ball into run of player C. C finishes drill with long diagonal back to starting position.
INSTRUCTIONS:	Start drill of with 2 touches.
COACHING POINTS:	• Accurate passing (correct direction and pace). • Quick movement after the pass. • Communication.

OBJECTIVE:	Improving passing on the dribble
NUMBER OF PLAYERS:	6-10
AREA/FIELD:	20 yards x 25 yards
TIME:	10-15 minutes
EQUIPMENT:	4 cones, supply of balls

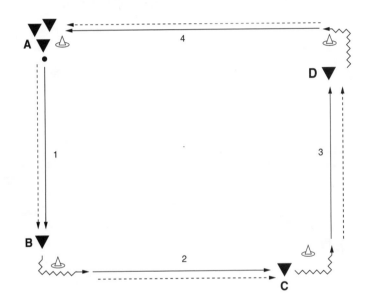

ORGANIZATION:	Player A passes to B, Player B receives ball and dribbles around cone. After dribble pass to player C. Drill continues same way back to starting position.
COACHING POINTS:	• Initial movement away from ball before receiving ball. • Eye contact and communication. • Pass to feet. • Quick turn and dribble.
VARIATIONS:	Start drill with 2 balls (player A and C).

COMBINATION PLAY   8

OBJECTIVE:	Improving combination play, movement off ball
NUMBER OF PLAYERS:	6-12 players
AREA/FIELD:	20 yards x 25 yards
TIME:	15-20 minutes
EQUIPMENT:	4 cones, supply of balls

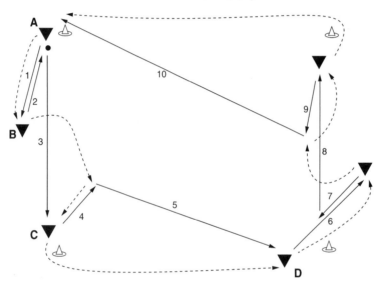

ORGANIZATION:
- Player A plays wall pass with player B. After wall pass A passes to player C. C passes ball to player B who made run.
- Player B passes long to player D. Drill starts again with player D.

INSTRUCTIONS: Start drill slow so players know where to go/run and pass.

COACHING POINTS:
- Movement off and on ball.
- Immediate movement after pass.
- Accurate passing.

VARIATIONS: Introduce defenders.

OBJECTIVE: Improving attacking patterns

NUMBER OF PLAYERS: 14-20

AREA/FIELD: Half field

TIME: 30-40 minutes

EQUIPMENT: 2 goals, cone, supply of balls

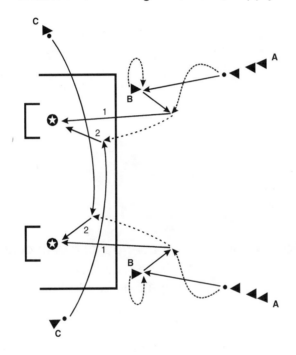

ORGANIZATION: A: Player 1 passes to player 2 for wall pass. Follow pass and shoot on goal. After shot quick run to endline.

B: Same as A: After shot on goal finish cross from flank.

INSTRUCTIONS: Players switch positions after pass or shot.

COACHING POINTS: • Quick, crisp passing.
• Passes into run of receiving players.

COMBINATION PLAY   10

OBJECTIVE:	Learning attacking patterns
NUMBER OF PLAYERS:	5-15
AREA/FIELD:	Half field
TIME:	15-20 minutes
EQUIPMENT:	Supply of balls

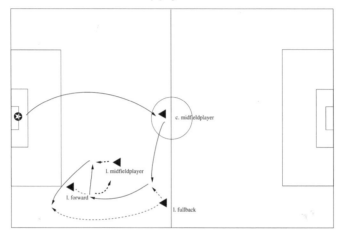

ORGANIZATION:	Goalkeeper punts ball to central midfielder. Midfielder receives ball and passes ball to fullback. Fullback plays ball to forward. Forward plays ball to midfielder. Fullback makes overlapping run and receives ball from midfielder. Fullback crosses ball to forward and midfielder in front of goal.
INSTRUCTIONS:	Start off using 2 touches, go to one touch play.
COACHING POINTS:	• Movement before and after pass. • Accurate passing into run. • Eye contact and communication.
VARIATIONS:	• Introduce defenders. • Introduce more attacking players.

COMBINATION PLAY   11

OBJECTIVE:	Learning attacking patterns
NUMBER OF PLAYERS:	5-15 players
AREA/FIELD:	Half field
TIME:	15-20 minutes
EQUIPMENT:	Supply of balls

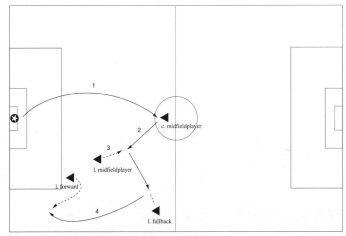

ORGANIZATION: Goalkeeper punts ball to central midfielder who receives ball and plays ball to other midfielder. He passes to fullback on the flank. Fullback plays a long ball down the flank to forward. Forward crosses ball to midfielder and fullback in front of goal.

INSTRUCTIONS: Start off using 2 touches, go to one touch play.

COACHING POINTS:
• Movement on and off ball.
• Passes into run.
• Pass ball at correct pace and at correct foot.

VARIATIONS:
• Introduce defenders.
• Introduce more attacking players.

COMBINATION PLAY   12

OBJECTIVE:	Learning attacking patterns
NUMBER OF PLAYERS:	4-15
AREA/FIELD:	Half field
TIME:	15-20 minutes
EQUIPMENT:	Supply of balls

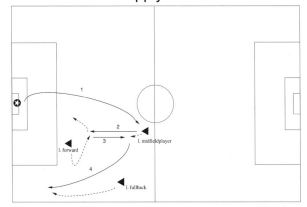

ORGANIZATION:	Goalkeeper punts ball to central midfielder. Midfielder receives ball and plays a 1-2 combination with forward. After receiving back ball from forward, midfielder plays a long pass to flank to fullback. Back crosses ball to forward and midfielder in front of goal.
INSTRUCTIONS:	Start off using 2 touch, go to one touch play.
COACHING POINTS:	• Initial movement away from ball by forward to create space. • Pass at correct pace and correct foot. • Eye contact and communication between all players.
VARIATIONS:	• Introduce defenders. • Introduce more attacking players.

COMBINATION PLAY   13

OBJECTIVE:	Learning attacking patterns
NUMBER OF PLAYERS:	6-15
AREA/FIELD:	Half field
TIME:	15-20 minutes
EQUIPMENT:	Supply of ball

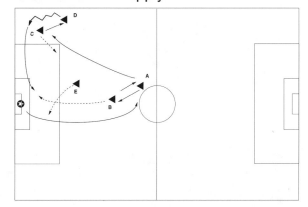

ORGANIZATION: Goalkeeper punts ball to player A. Player A and B play a quick 1-2 combination. Player A passes to flank to player C. Player C lays ball off to Player D who dribbles to end line and crosses ball to players B and E in front of goal.

INSTRUCTIONS: Let players switch positions frequently.

COACHING POINTS:
- Concentration on passes and crosses.
- Use both flanks for crosses and runs.
- Correct pace on passes and crosses.
- Crossover runs by Players B and E (far and near post).
- Play 1 touch as much as possible.

VARIATIONS:
- Introduce defenders.
- Introduce more attacking players.

COMBINATION PLAY   14

OBJECTIVE:	Learning attacking patterns
NUMBER OF PLAYERS:	10-18
AREA/FIELD:	Half field
TIME:	15-20 minutes
EQUIPMENT:	Supply of balls

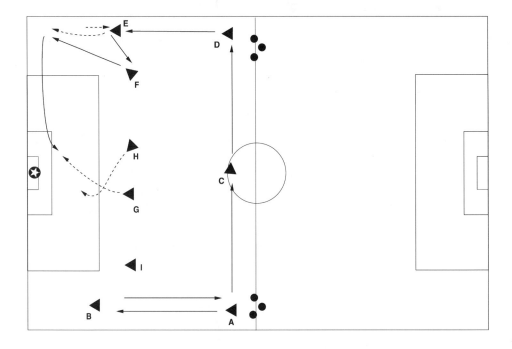

ORGANIZATION: Player A and B play long 1-2 combination. Player A switches point of attack via player C to Player D. D Plays ball to E. Player E plays ball to F who passes ball back into E's run down the flank. Player E crosses ball to players H and G.

INSTRUCTIONS: Play can start from either side of the field.

COMBINATION PLAY   14

COACHING POINTS:
- Switch point of attack quickly.
- Play one touch as much as possible.
- Accurate passing.
- Intelligent movement off the ball to create space and options.
- Crossover runs by players H and G in front of goal.
- Determination inside box to score on goal.

VARIATIONS:
- Introduce defenders.
- Introduce more attacking players in front of goal.

COMBINATION PLAY   15

OBJECTIVE:	Learning attacking patterns
NUMBER OF PLAYERS:	8-18
AREA/FIELD:	Half field
TIME:	15-20 minutes
EQUIPMENT:	Supply of balls

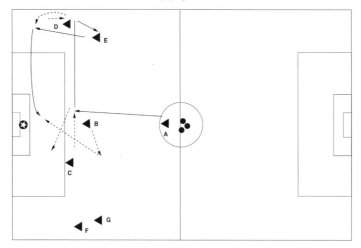

ORGANIZATION:
- Player A passes to player C (after crossover runs by B and C).
- Player B passes ball to flank player D. D plays short combination with E and crosses ball to players B and C in front of goal.

INSTRUCTIONS:
- Play drill over both flanks.
- Let players switch positions.

COACHING POINTS:
- Initial movement off ball before receiving pass.
- Accurate passing.
- Crossover runs by Players B and C.
- Communication between all players.

VARIATIONS:
- Introduce defenders.
- Introduce more attacking players.

COMBINATION PLAY 16

OBJECTIVE:	Improving passing and crossing in attacking patterns
NUMBER OF PLAYERS:	10-16
AREA/FIELD:	Half field
TIME:	15 minutes
EQUIPMENT:	Supply of balls

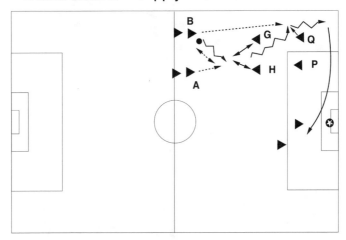

ORGANIZATION:	• Player A or B play ball to player G or H. G or H play wallpass back to player A or B. • Player A or B pass ball to flank to player P or Q who turns and crosses ball to 2 forwards in front of goal.
INSTRUCTIONS:	• Drill can be executed from both sides of field. • Let players switch positions.
COACHING POINTS:	• Quick and crisp passing. • Passes at correct pace and correct foot. • Movement before the pass.
VARIATIONS:	Introduce defenders.

COMBINATION PLAY   17

OBJECTIVE:	Improving attacking over flank/wing
NUMBER OF PLAYERS:	14-18
AREA/FIELD:	Half field
TIME:	15 minutes
EQUIPMENT:	Supply of balls

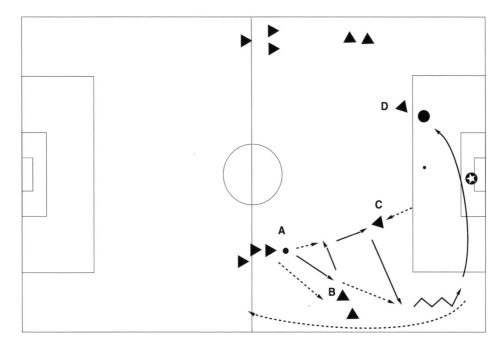

ORGANIZATION:	• Player A plays 1-2 combination with player B. After pass player B makes run to flank.
	• Player A passes to player C who passes to player B on flank. Player B dribbles to end line and crosses ball to forward in front of goal.
INSTRUCTIONS:	• Let players switch positions.
	• Defender in front of goal.
	• Alternate sides for drill.

COACHING POINTS: • After pass to flank player C becomes second forward with player D (cross-over runs).
• Quick combinations on ground.
• Movement before and after pass.

VARIATIONS: Introduce more defenders.

COMBINATION PLAY 18

OBJECTIVE:	Learning to execute a fast counter attack
NUMBER OF PLAYERS:	6-14
AREA/FIELD:	Full field
TIME:	20 minutes
EQUIPMENT:	Supply of balls

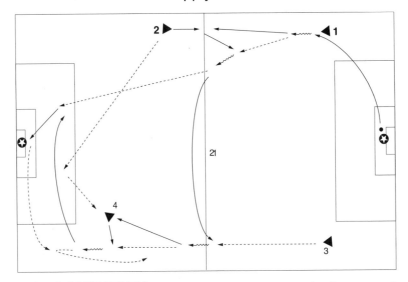

ORGANIZATION:
- Goalkeeper throws ball out to player 1. Player 1 dribbles forward and passes ball to player 2 for a 1-2 combination. After receiving back ball from 2, player 1 dribbles toward middle of field and passes to opposite flank to player 3 who made a run from a back position.
- Player 3 dribbles forward with ball and plays a 1-2 combination with player 4. After receiving pass back from 4 he crosses ball to player 1 and 2 in front of goal.

COMBINATION PLAY   18

INSTRUCTIONS: Start drill from opposite side after cross
                        and finish on goal.

COACHING POINTS: • Execute everything at game speed.
                        • Accurate passing into run.
                        • Correct pace on ball.

VARIATIONS: Introduce defenders.

OBJECTIVE: Learning to finish from crosses from flank/wing

NUMBER OF PLAYERS: 10-16

AREA/FIELD: Half field

TIME: 20 minutes

EQUIPMENT: Supply of balls

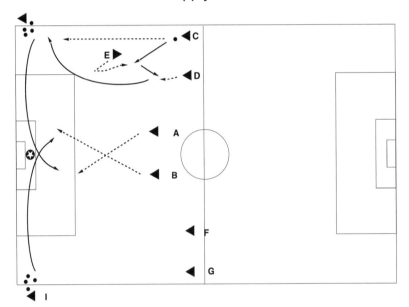

ORGANIZATION: Player C plays ball to player E who plays ball back to player D. D plays a long pass down the flank to player C. Player C crosses ball to players A and B in front of goal. After cross has been finished, player on opposite flank crosses ball for second finish on goal by players A and B.

INSTRUCTIONS:
• Drill should be alternated from left to right.
• Let players switch to different positions.

COMBINATION PLAY   19

COACHING POINTS:
- Intelligent movement before and after pass.
- Initial movement away from ball to create space.
- Accurate passing.
- Concentration.

VARIATIONS: Introduce defenders.

COMBINATION PLAY   20

OBJECTIVE: Improving combination play with finishing on goal

NUMBER OF PLAYERS: 10-14

AREA/FIELD: Half field

TIME: 20 minutes

EQUIPMENT: 2 cones, supply of balls

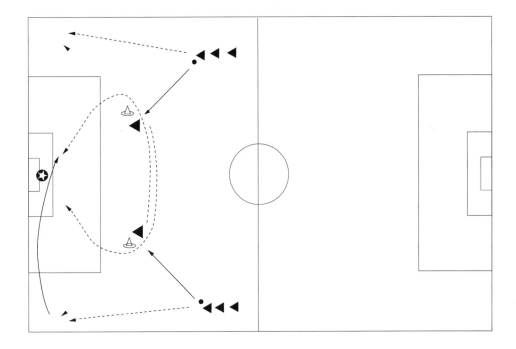

ORGANIZATION: Player 1 plays long combination with player 2. Run down flank by player and cross to two forwards in front of goal.

INSTRUCTIONS: Alternate sides for drill.

COMBINATION PLAY   21

OBJECTIVE: Improving combination play with finish on goal

NUMBER OF PLAYERS: 12-18

AREA/FIELD: Half field

TIME: 20 minutes

EQUIPMENT: 2 cones, supply of balls

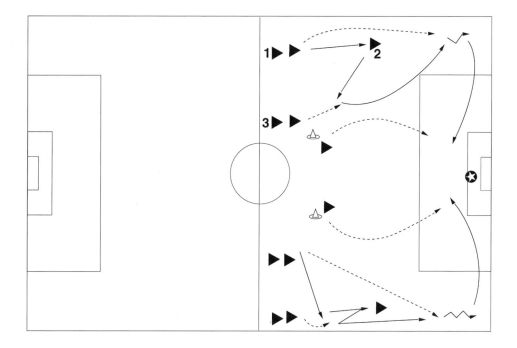

ORGANIZATION: Player 1 passes ball to player 2 who passes inside to player 3. Player 3 plays ball to flank into player 1's run. Player 1 dribbles to end line and crosses ball to 2 forwards.

INSTRUCTIONS: • Players 1, 2 and 3 can use different combinations before passing to flank.
• Alternate sides for drill.

COMBINATION PLAY   22

OBJECTIVE: Learning attacking patterns

NUMBER OF PLAYERS: 8-14

AREA/FIELD: Half field

TIME: 20 minutes

EQUIPMENT: 2 cones, supply of balls

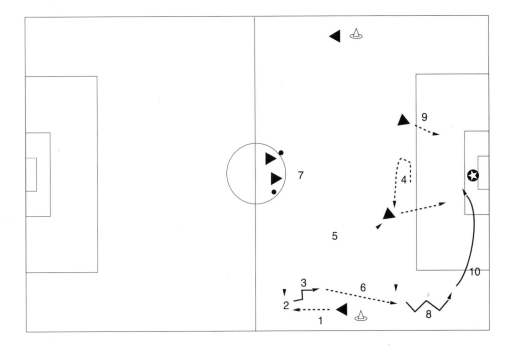

ORGANIZATION: Pass from midfielder to flank/wing. Player on flank receives pass and cuts inside to play combination with forward. Forward plays ball to corner where flank player receives ball, dribbles inside and crosses ball to two forwards.

INSTRUCTIONS: • Let players switch positions.
• Execute drill from both flanks.

COMBINATION PLAY 23

OBJECTIVE: Practicing attacking patterns

NUMBER OF PLAYERS: 7-14

AREA/FIELD: Half field

TIME: 20 minutes

EQUIPMENT: 2 cones, supply of balls

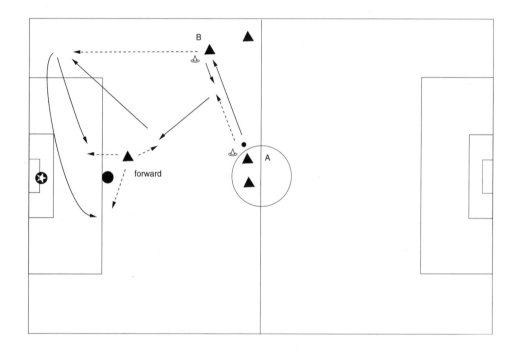

ORGANIZATION: Players A and B play long 1-2 combination. After A receives ball back from B, he plays ball to forward. Forward passes ball down the wing to player B. B crosses ball to forward inside box (with defender).

INSTRUCTIONS: Let players switch positions.

COMBINATION PLAY　　24

OBJECTIVE:	Improving finishing on goal
NUMBER OF PLAYERS:	4-10
AREA:	Half field
TIME:	20 minutes
EQUIPMENT:	Supply of balls

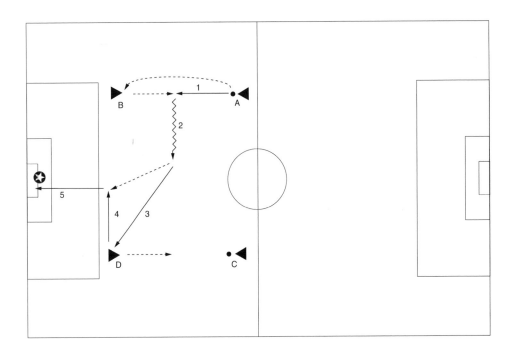

ORGANIZATION:	Player A passes ball to player B. B receives ball and turns inside for dribble. On the dribble player B passes to player D who plays ball square for B to take shot on goal.
INSTRUCTIONS:	Start same drill on left side of field.

COMBINATION PLAY   25

OBJECTIVE:	Improving finishing on goal
NUMBER OF PLAYERS:	4-10
AREA/FIELD:	Half field
TIME:	20 minutes
EQUIPMENT:	Supply of balls

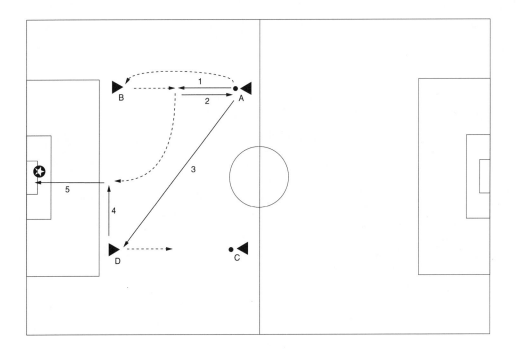

ORGANIZATION: Players A and B play 1-2 combination. After receiving back ball, player A passes diagonal to player D. Player D plays ball square for player B to finish on goal.

INSTRUCTIONS: Let players switch position after each shot.

COMBINATION PLAY 26

OBJECTIVE:	Improving finishing on goal
NUMBER OF PLAYERS:	4-10
AREA/FIELD:	Half field
TIME:	20 minutes
EQUIPMENT:	Supply of balls

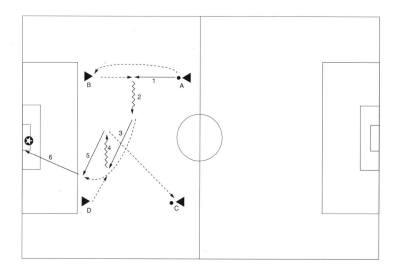

ORGANIZATION:	Player A passes ball to B. B cuts ball inside and dribbles toward player D. Pass to player D who dribbles while player B overlaps. Player D passes ball into B's run who shoots on goal.
INSTRUCTIONS:	Let players switch positions after each shot.

OBJECTIVE:	Improving finishing on goal
NUMBER OF PLAYERS:	4-10
AREA/FIELD:	Half field
TIME:	20 minutes
EQUIPMENT:	Supply of balls

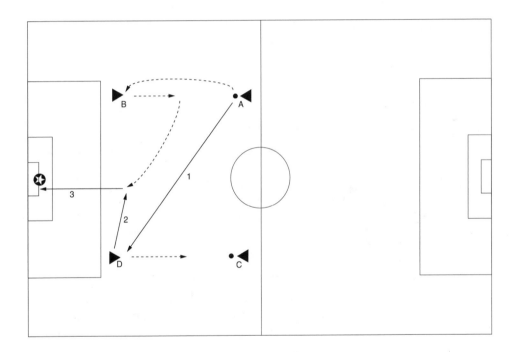

ORGANIZATION:	Player passes long (diagonal) to player D. Player D lays off ball square to Player B (after movement toward player A) who shoots on goal.
INSTRUCTIONS:	• Let players switch positions after each shot. • Alternate sides for drill.

COMBINATION PLAY   28

OBJECTIVE:	Improving attacking patterns
NUMBER OF PLAYERS:	10-16
AREA/FIELD:	Half field
TIME:	20 minutes
EQUIPMENT:	Supply of balls

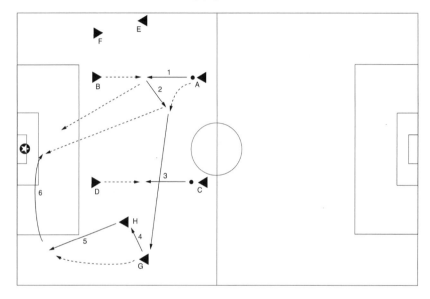

ORGANIZATION: Player A plays 1-2 combination with B. After combination he plays diagonal pass to player G. G plays 1-2 combination with H and makes run down the wing. G receives ball and crosses ball to players A and B in front of goal.

INSTRUCTIONS: After finish on goal, player C starts drill on opposite side.

COACHING POINTS:
• Pass ball to flank in front of player to maintain speed (into run).
• Cross ball one time or dribble to end-line before crossing.

- Cross ball out of reach of goalkeeper.
- Vary crosses; long, short, driven, in or outswinging, high or low.
- Eye contact between player crossing and players in front of goal.
- Players need to make cross-over runs in front of goal.
- Players in front of goal need to be aggressive going for ball.
- Players in front of goal have to be in motion, not stationary.
- Make runs and passes at the correct time.
- Score.

COMBINATION PLAY   29

OBJECTIVE:	Improving attacking patterns
NUMBER OF PLAYERS:	14-18
AREA/FIELD:	Full field
TIME:	20-25 minutes
EQUIPMENT:	Supply of balls

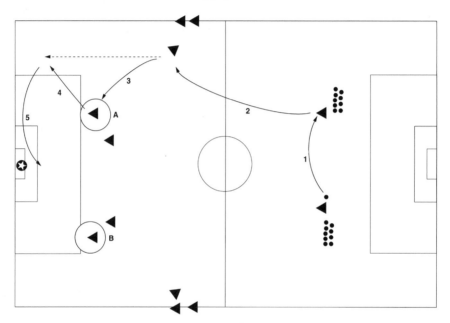

ORGANIZATION:	Long ball across field followed by long pass to flank. Player on flank receives ball and plays ball to forward A who passes to corner. Player on flank runs on to pass in the corner and crosses ball to 2 forwards in front of goal.
INSTRUCTIONS:	Drill can be started on either side of field.
COACHING POINTS:	• Pass ball to flank in front of player to maintain speed (into run). • Cross ball one time or dribble to end-line before crossing.

- Cross ball out of reach of goalkeeper.
- Vary crosses; long, short, driven, in or outswinging, high or low.
- Eye contact between player crossing and players in front of goal.
- Players need to make crossover runs in front of goal.
- Players in front of goal need to be aggressive going for ball.
- Players in front of goal have to be in motion, not stationary.
- Make runs and passes at the correct time.
- Score.

COMBINATION PLAY   30

OBJECTIVE: Improving attacking patterns (build from back)

NUMBER OF PLAYERS: 14-18

AREA/FIELD: Full field

TIME: 20 minutes

EQUIPMENT: Supply of balls

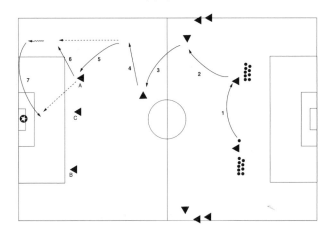

ORGANIZATION: Long combinations to work ball up field to forward A . Player A plays ball to corner where overlapping player receives ball and crosses to 3 forwards in front of goal.

INSTRUCTIONS:
- Drill can be executed from both sides of field.
- Let players switch positions.

COACHING POINTS:
- Pass ball to flank in front of player to maintain speed (into run).
- Cross ball one time or dribble to end-line before crossing.
- Cross ball out of reach of goalkeeper.
- Vary crosses; long, short, driven, in or outswinging, high or low.

- Eye contact between player crossing and players in front of goal.
- Players need to make crossover runs in front of goal.
- Players in front of goal need to be aggressive going for ball.
- Players in front of goal have to be in motion, not stationary.
- Make runs and passes at the correct time.
- Score.

OBJECTIVE: Improving attacking patterns (build from back)

NUMBER OF PLAYERS: 14-18

AREA/FIELD: Full field

TIME: 20 minutes

EQUIPMENT: Supply of balls

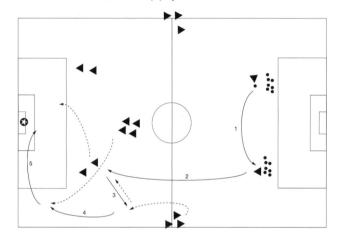

ORGANIZATION: Square pass to change field. Long ball from back to forward. Forward plays ball to outside to midfielder. Midfielder plays ball to corner to overlapping central midfielder or forward. Cross to forwards in front of goal.

COACHING POINTS:
- Pass ball to flank in front of player to maintain speed (into run).
- Cross ball one time or dribble to end-line before crossing.
- Cross ball out of reach of goalkeeper.
- Vary crosses; long, short, driven, in or outswinging, high or low.
- Eye contact between player crossing and players in front of goal.

- Players need to make crossover runs in front of goal.
- Players in front of goal need to be aggressive going for ball.
- Players in front of goal have to be in motion, not stationary.
- Make runs and passes at the correct time.
- Score.

COMBINATION PLAY   32

OBJECTIVE:	Improving attacking patterns (build from back)
NUMBER OF PLAYERS:	14-18
AREA/FIELD:	Full field
TIME:	20 minutes
EQUIPMENT:	Supply of balls

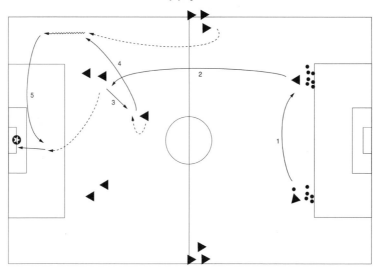

ORGANIZATION: Square pass to change field. Long ball from back to forward. Forward lays ball off to centrally located player who passes to flank. Overlapping flank player receives ball, dribbles to endline and crosses ball to 2 forwards inside box.

COACHING POINTS:

- Pass ball to flank in front of player to maintain speed (into run).
- Cross ball one time or dribble to endline before crossing.
- Cross ball out of reach of goalkeeper.
- Vary crosses; long, short, driven, in or outswinging, high or low.

- Eye contact between player crossing and players in front of goal.
- Players need to make crossover runs in front of goal.
- Players in front of goal need to be aggressive going for ball.
- Players in front of goal have to be in motion, not stationary.
- Make runs and passes at the correct time.
- Score.

COMBINATION PLAY   33

OBJECTIVE:	Improving attacking patterns (build from back)
NUMBER OF PLAYERS:	14-18
AREA/FIELD:	Full field
TIME:	20 minutes
EQUIPMENT:	Supply of balls

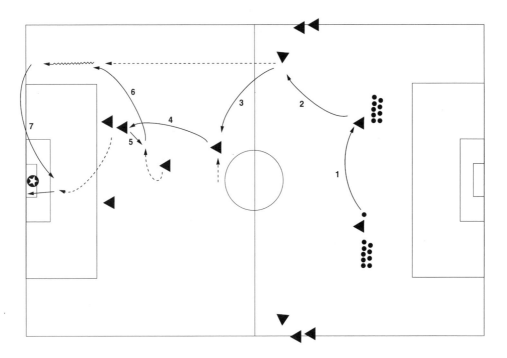

ORGANIZATION: Square ball to change point of attack. Long ball from back to flank. Flank player plays diagonal ball to central midfielder. Midfielder passes ball to forward. Forward plays quick 1-2 combination with other midfielder who plays ball to corner to overlapping flank player. Flank player crosses ball to 2 forwards inside box.

COACHING POINTS:

- Pass ball to flank in front of player to maintain speed (into run).
- Cross ball one time or dribble to end-line before crossing.
- Cross ball out of reach of goalkeeper.
- Vary crosses; long, short, driven, in or outswinging, high or low.
- Eye contact between player crossing and players in front of goal.
- Players need to make crossover runs in front of goal.
- Players in front of goal need to be aggressive going for ball.
- Players in front of goal have to be in motion, not stationary.
- Make runs and passes at the correct time.
- Score.

COMBINATION PLAY   34

OBJECTIVE:	Improving attacking patterns (build from back)
NUMBER OF PLAYERS:	14-18
AREA/FIELD:	Full field
TIME:	20 minutes
EQUIPMENT:	Supply of balls

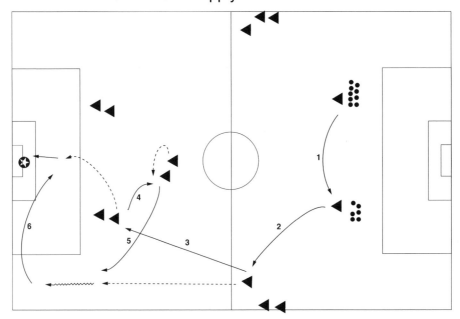

ORGANIZATION:	Square ball to change point of attack. Long ball from back to flank player. Flank player plays long ball to forward. Forward plays ball inside to central midfielder who passes to overlapping flank player. Flank player crosses ball inside box to 2 forwards.
COACHING POINTS:	• Pass ball to flank in front of player to maintain speed (into run).
	• Cross ball one time or dribble to end-line before crossing.

- Cross ball out of reach of goalkeeper.
- Vary crosses; long, short, driven, in or outswinging, high or low.
- Eye contact between player crossing and players in front of goal.
- Players need to make crossover runs in front of goal.
- Players in front of goal need to be aggressive going for ball.
- Players in front of goal have to be in motion, not stationary.
- Make runs and passes at the correct time.
- Score.

OBJECTIVE:	Improving attacking patterns (build from back)
NUMBER OF PLAYERS:	14-18
AREA/FIELD:	Full field
TIME:	20 minutes
EQUIPMENT:	Supply of balls

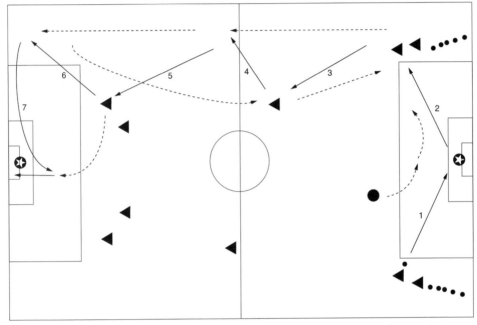

ORGANIZATION:	Pass back to goalkeeper who switches play to opposite side. Player receiving ball plays a long 1-2 combination with midfielder. After receiving pass back from midfielder he passes long to forward and continues run down flank. Forward passes to corner, cross to two forwards inside box.
COACHING POINTS:	• Pass ball to flank in front of player to maintain speed (into run).

- Cross ball one time or dribble to end-line before crossing.
- Cross ball out of reach of goalkeeper.
- Vary crosses; long, short, driven, in or outswinging, high or low.
- Eye contact between player crossing and players in front of goal.
- Players need to make crossover runs in front of goal.
- Players in front of goal need to be aggressive going for ball.
- Players in front of goal have to be in motion, not stationary.
- Make runs and passes at the correct time.
- Score.

COMBINATION PLAY   36

OBJECTIVE:	Improving attacking patterns (build from back)
NUMBER OF PLAYERS:	14-18
AREA/FIELD:	Full field
TIME:	25 minutes
EQUIPMENT:	Supply of balls

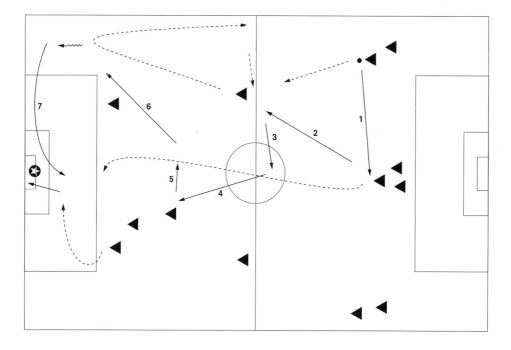

ORGANIZATION: Central defender receives pass from fullback. Central defender passes long to midfielder for 1-2 combination. After receiving back pass he plays 1-2 combination with forward and passes to the corner where midfielder has made run to. Midfielder crosses ball inside box to 2 forwards and central defender.

COMBINATION PLAY   36

COACHING POINTS:

- Pass ball to flank in front of player to maintain speed (into run).
- Cross ball one time or dribble to end-line before crossing.
- Cross ball out of reach of goalkeeper.
- Vary crosses; long, short, driven, in or outswinging, high or low.
- Eye contact between player crossing and players in front of goal.
- Players need to make crossover runs in front of goal.
- Players in front of goal need to be aggressive going for ball.
- Players in front of goal have to be in motion, not stationary.
- Make runs and passes at the correct time.
- Score.

COMBINATION PLAY   37

OBJECTIVE:	Improving attacking patterns (build from back)
NUMBER OF PLAYERS:	12-18
AREA/FIELD:	Full field
TIME:	20 minutes
EQUIPMENT:	Supply of balls

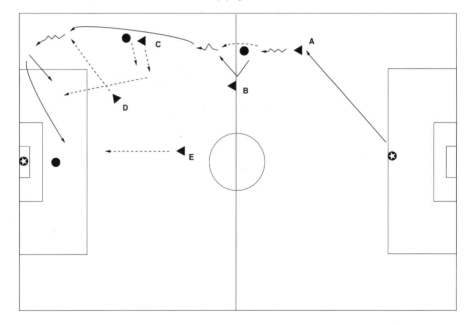

ORGANIZATION:
- Goalkeeper punts/throws ball to player A. Player A dribbles towards defender and goes around defender by using player B for wall pass. After receiving back pass he plays ball deep to corner for player D (player C makes run inside to draw away defender).
- Player D crosses the ball to player C on top of 18 yard box or to far post to player E.

COACHING POINTS:
- Pass ball to flank in front of player to maintain speed (into run).
- Cross ball one time or dribble to end-line before crossing.
- Cross ball out of reach of goalkeeper.
- Vary crosses; long, short, driven, in or outswinging, high or low.
- Eye contact between player crossing and players in front of goal.
- Players need to make crossover runs in front of goal.
- Players in front of goal need to be aggressive going for ball.
- Players in front of goal have to be in motion, not stationary.
- Make runs and passes at the correct time.
- Score.

COMBINATION PLAY   38

OBJECTIVE:	Improving attacking patterns
NUMBER OF PLAYERS:	5-15
AREA/FIELD:	Half field
TIME:	20 minutes
EQUIPMENT:	Supply of balls

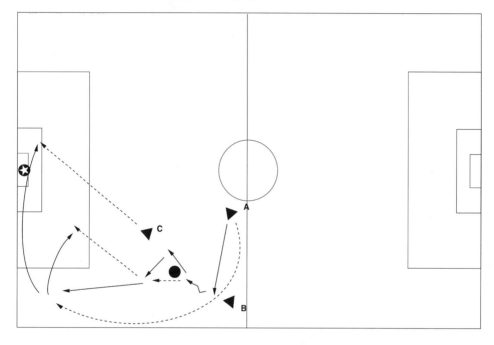

ORGANIZATION:

• Player A passes ball to player B and overlaps. Player B dribbles toward defender and plays 1-2 combination with player C. After receiving back pass, player B passes ball to player A in corner.

• Player A crosses ball to player C or plays ball back to player B.

INSTRUCTIONS: When attackers loose possession, they must pressure ball immediately.

COMBINATION PLAY   38

COACHING POINTS:
- Pass ball to flank in front of player to maintain speed (into run).
- Cross ball one time or dribble to end-line before crossing.
- Cross ball out of reach of goalkeeper.
- Vary crosses; long, short, driven, in or outswinging, high or low.
- Eye contact between player crossing and players in front of goal.
- Players need to make crossover runs in front of goal.
- Players in front of goal need to be aggressive going for ball.
- Players in front of goal have to be in motion, not stationary.
- Make runs and passes at the correct time.
- Score.

OBJECTIVE: Improving attacking patterns

NUMBER OF PLAYERS: 10-16

AREA/FIELD: Two-thirds of field

TIME: 20 minutes

EQUIPMENT: 2 goals, supply of balls

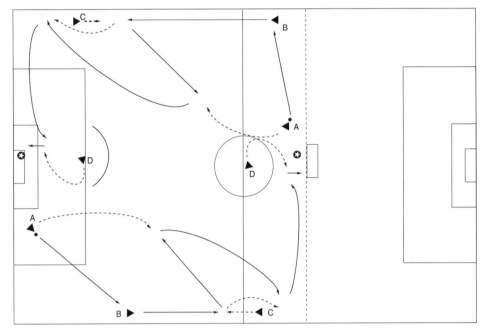

ORGANIZATION: Player A passes ball to player B who plays to player C. Player C passes ball into run of player A who plays back to C in corner. Player C crosses ball to D who finishes on goal.

INSTRUCTIONS: Same drill on both sides of field.

COACHING POINTS:
- Pass ball to flank in front of player to maintain speed (into run).
- Cross ball one time or dribble to end-line before crossing.

- Cross ball out of reach of goalkeeper.
- Vary crosses; long, short, driven, in or outswinging, high or low.
- Eye contact between player crossing and players in front of goal.
- Players need to make crossover runs in front of goal.
- Players in front of goal need to be aggressive going for ball.
- Players in front of goal have to be in motion, not stationary.
- Make runs and passes at the correct time.
- Score.

COMBINATION PLAY   40

OBJECTIVE:	Improving attacking patterns
NUMBER OF PLAYERS:	14-18
AREA/FIELD:	Half field
TIME:	20 minutes
EQUIPMENT:	2 goals, supply of balls

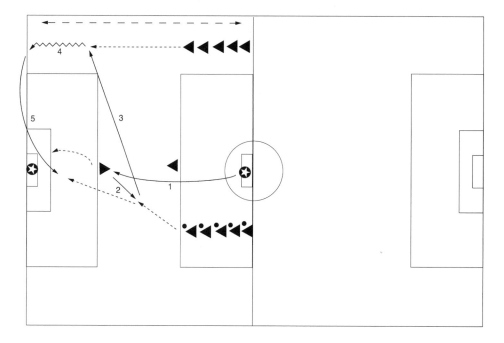

ORGANIZATION:	Goalkeeper throws/punts ball to forward who plays ball short to midfielder on side. Midfielder passes ball to opposite flank to flank player. Player on flank dribbles to end line and crosses ball to players in front of goal.
INSTRUCTIONS:	Let players switch positions frequently.
COACHING POINTS:	• Pass ball to flank in front of player to maintain speed (into run).

- Cross ball one time or dribble to end-line before crossing.
- Cross ball out of reach of goalkeeper.
- Vary crosses; long, short, driven, in or outswinging, high or low.
- Eye contact between player crossing and players in front of goal.
- Players need to make crossover runs in front of goal.
- Players in front of goal need to be aggressive going for ball.
- Players in front of goal have to be in motion, not stationary.
- Make runs and passes at the correct time.
- Score.

COMBINATION PLAY 41

OBJECTIVE: Utilizing space on flanks to create scoring chances

NUMBER OF PLAYERS: 12-18

AREA/FIELD: Half field

TIME: 20 minutes

EQUIPMENT: 2 goals, supply of balls

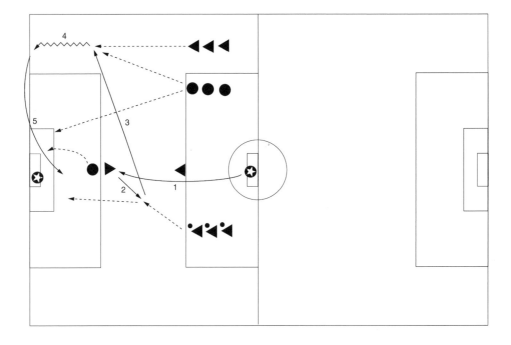

ORGANIZATION: Goalkeeper throws ball to forward who checks to ball. After receiving pass forward passes ball to flank. Player receives ball and cross passes ball to opposite flank. Player on opposite flank makes run to receive pass, dribbles and crosses ball into box.

COMBINATION PLAY   41

INSTRUCTIONS:
- A defender on flank will put pressure on flank player or goes inside box to defend cross.
- A 2v2 situation inside box is created.
- When defenders win ball they can score on goal in midfield.

COACHING POINTS:
- Crisp, hard passing.
- Play 1 or 2 touch.
- Movement before pass.
- Don't be stationary receiving pass or cross.
- Quick transition when ball is lost/won.

COMBINATION PLAY   42

OBJECTIVE: Improving scoring and quick transition

NUMBER OF PLAYERS: 14

AREA/FIELD: Half field

TIME: 20 minutes

EQUIPMENT: 2 cones, supply of balls

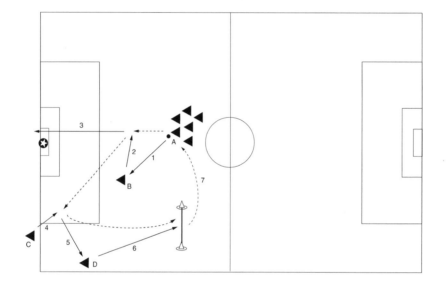

ORGANIZATION: Players A and B play 1-2 combination and A shoots on goal. After shot player A makes run to corner to play a combination with players C and D. Player D receives ball and passes ball through cones to A who runs on.

INSTRUCTIONS:
- Start drill right after shot on goal.
- Play direct.
- Concentration on shots and passes.

VARIATIONS: Introduce defenders.

COACHING POINTS:
- Crisp, hard passing.
- Play 1 or 2 touch.

COMBINATION PLAY   **43**

OBJECTIVE:	Improving scoring from pass and after cross
NUMBER OF PLAYERS:	20
AREA/FIELD:	Half field
TIME:	20 minutes
EQUIPMENT:	1 cone, 2 goals, supply of balls

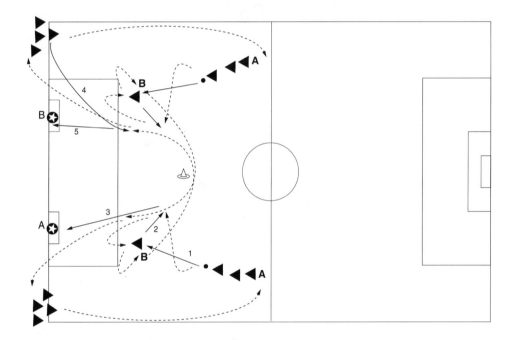

ORGANIZATION:	Player A and B play 1-2 combination and player shoots on goal. After shot player A sprints around cone and finishes cross from far corner.
INSTRUCTIONS:	Drill is started on both sides.
COACHING POINTS:	• Play direct. • Play balls into run.

COMBINATION PLAY   44

OBJECTIVE:	Practicing building up over flanks
NUMBER OF PLAYERS:	12-18
AREA/FIELD	Half field
TIME:	25
EQUIPMENT:	2 cones, 2 small goals, supply of balls.

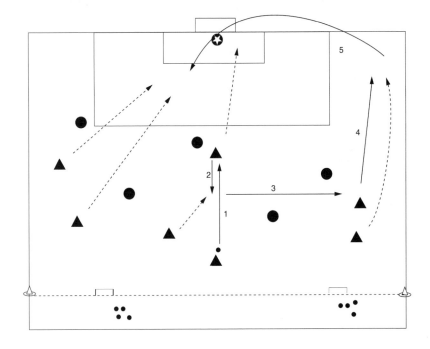

ORGANIZATION:	• Game of 7v5. Attacking teams utilizes numerical advantage to build up over flank, and tries to score on goal with goalkeeper. • Defending team can score on small goals.
INSTRUCTIONS:	• Start game with attacking team each time a team scores. • Start game by passing to forward first before passing to flank.

COACHING POINTS

- Pass ball to flank in front of player to maintain speed (into run).
- Cross ball one time or dribble to end-line before crossing.
- Cross ball out of reach of goalkeeper.
- Vary crosses; long, short, driven, in or outswinging, high or low.
- Eye contact between player crossing and players in front of goal.
- Players need to make crossover runs in front of goal.
- Players in front of goal need to be aggressive going for ball.
- Players in front of goal have to be in motion, not stationary.
- Make runs and passes at the correct time.
- Score.

COMBINATION PLAY   45

OBJECTIVE:	Practicing building up over flanks
NUMBER OF PLAYERS:	12-18
AREA/FIELD:	Half field
TIME:	30
EQUIPMENT:	2 cones, 2 small goals, supply of balls.

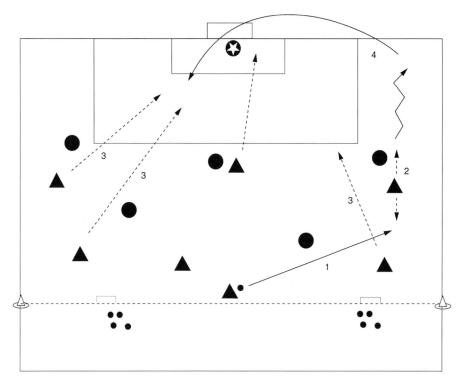

ORGANIZATION:	• Game of 7v5. Attacking teams utilizes numerical advantage to build up over flank, and tries to score on goal with goalkeeper.
	• Defending team can score on small goals.
INSTRUCTIONS:	Start game with first pass to flank player.

COACHING POINTS:

- Pass ball to flank in front of player to maintain speed (into run).
- Cross ball one time or dribble to end-line before crossing.
- Cross ball out of reach of goalkeeper.
- Vary crosses; long, short, driven, in or outswinging, high or low.
- Eye contact between player crossing and players in front of goal.
- Players need to make crossover runs in front of goal.
- Players in front of goal need to be aggressive going for ball.
- Players in front of goal have to be in motion, not stationary.
- Make runs and passes at the correct time.
- Score.

OBJECTIVE:	Game of 7v5 plus 1 neutral player.
NUMBER OF PLAYERS:	12-18
AREA/FIELD:	Half field
TIME:	30 minutes
EQUIPMENT:	2 cones, 2 small goals, supply of balls.

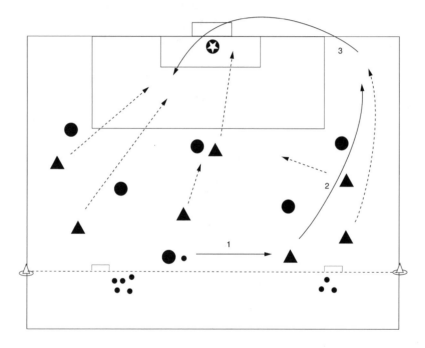

ORGANIZATION:
- Game of 7v5. Attacking team utilizes numerical advantage to build up over flank, and tries to score on goal with goalkeeper.
- Defending team can score on small goals.

INSTRUCTIONS:
- Game starts with ball from neutral player to attackers.
- Neutral player plays on team with possession to create 8v5 or 7v6.

COACHING POINTS:

- Pass ball to flank in front of player to maintain speed (into run).
- Cross ball one time or dribble to end-line before crossing.
- Cross ball out of reach of goalkeeper.
- Vary crosses; long, short, driven, in or outswinging, high or low.
- Eye contact between player crossing and players in front of goal.
- Players need to make crossover runs in front of goal.
- Players in front of goal need to be aggressive going for ball.
- Players in front of goal have to be in motion, not stationary.
- Make runs and passes at the correct time.
- Score.

COMBINATION PLAY   47

OBJECTIVE:	Attacking over flank
NUMBER OF PLAYERS:	12-18
AREA/FIELD:	Half field
TIME:	20 minutes
EQUIPMENT:	Supply of balls

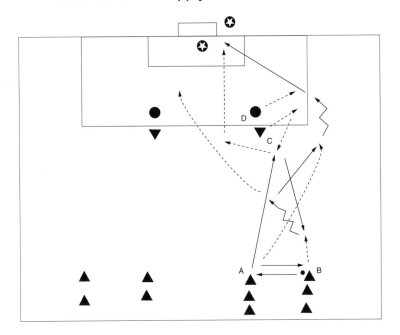

ORGANIZATION: Player A and B play short 1-2 combination before player A passes ball to forward C, C plays ball back to player B who dribbles inside. Player A makes overlapping run to flank and receives pass from player B. Player A takes ball toward 18 yard box and either shoots on goal or crosses ball to player B and C inside box for finish on goal.

INSTRUCTIONS: Repeat drill on other side.

COACHING POINTS:

- Pass ball to flank in front of player to maintain speed (into run).
- Cross ball one time or dribble to end-line before crossing.
- Cross ball out of reach of goalkeeper.
- Vary crosses; long, short, driven, in or outswinging, high or low.
- Eye contact between player crossing and players in front of goal.
- Players need to make crossover runs in front of goal.
- Players in front of goal need to be aggressive going for ball.
- Players in front of goal have to be in motion, not stationary.
- Make runs and passes at the correct time.
- Score.

COMBINATION PLAY 48

OBJECTIVE:	Creating scoring chances from build up in midfield
NUMBER OF PLAYERS:	14-18
AREA/FIELD:	Half field
TIME:	20-30 minutes
EQUIPMENT:	Supply of balls

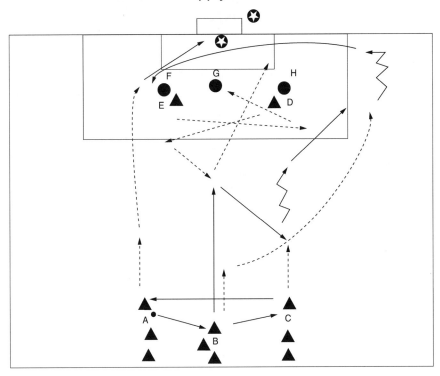

ORGANIZATION:	Player A, B and C exchange passes. Player B passes to forward D who passes back to player C. Player C dribbles toward box while player B overlaps. Player C passes to flank to player B. Player B crosses ball into box where a 4v3 situation is created.
INSTRUCTIONS:	Repeat drill on both sides.

COACHING POINTS:

- Pass ball to flank in front of player to maintain speed (into run).
- Cross ball one time or dribble to end-line before crossing.
- Cross ball out of reach of goalkeeper.
- Vary crosses; long, short, driven, in or outswinging, high or low.
- Eye contact between player crossing and players in front of goal.
- Players need to make crossover runs in front of goal.
- Players in front of goal need to be aggressive going for ball.
- Players in front of goal have to be in motion, not stationary.
- Make runs and passes at the correct time.
- Score.

COMBINATION PLAY   49

OBJECTIVE:	Practicing build up over flank using cross pass
NUMBER OF PLAYERS:	10
AREA/FIELD:	70 x 55 yards
TIME:	20-30 minutes
EQUIPMENT:	2 small goals, supply of balls

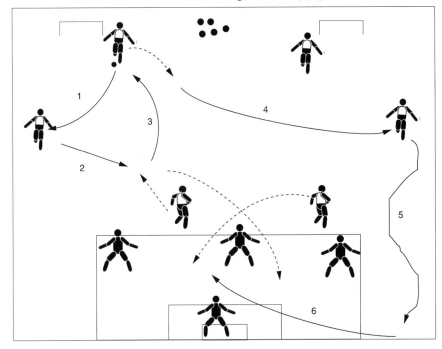

ORGANIZATION:	• Game of 6v3.
	• Attacking team can score on goal with goalkeeper. Defending team of 3 can score on 2 small goals.
INSTRUCTIONS:	Game starts on 1 side of field. Ball is passed till a cross pass to other side is possible. Player on opposite side will receive ball and cross ball inside box to teammates defended by 3 defenders.

COACHING POINTS:

- Pass ball to flank in front of player to maintain speed (into run).
- Cross ball one time or dribble to end-line before crossing.
- Cross ball out of reach of goalkeeper.
- Vary crosses; long, short, driven, in or outswinging, high or low.
- Eye contact between player crossing and players in front of goal.
- Players need to make crossover runs in front of goal.
- Players in front of goal need to be aggressive going for ball.
- Players in front of goal have to be in motion, not stationary.
- Make runs and passes at the correct time.
- Score.

COMBINATION PLAY 50

OBJECTIVE:	Improving build up by utilizing numerical advantage
NUMBER OF PLAYERS:	12
AREA/FIELD:	70 x 55 yards
TIME:	20-30 minutes
EQUIPMENT:	2 small goals, supply of balls

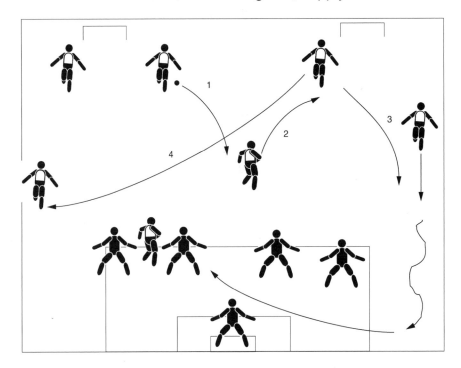

ORGANIZATION:	• Game of 7v4. • Attacking team will attempt to score on goal with goalkeeper. • Defending team can score on 2 small goals.
INSTRUCTIONS:	Use all attacking players in build up and finish off attack. Ball is passed until a cross pass from corner to other side is possible.

COACHING POINTS:
- Pass ball to flank in front of player to maintain speed (into run).
- Cross ball one time or dribble to end-line before crossing.
- Cross ball out of reach of goalkeeper.
- Vary crosses; long, short, driven, in or outswinging, high or low.
- Eye contact between player crossing and players in front of goal.
- Players need to make crossover runs in front of goal.
- Players in front of goal need to be aggressive going for ball.
- Players in front of goal have to be in motion, not stationary.
- Make runs and passes at the correct time.
- Score.

OBJECTIVE: Building attack from midfield over flanks

NUMBER OF PLAYERS: 18-20

AREA/FIELD: Full field

TIME: 30-40 minutes

EQUIPMENT: Supply of balls

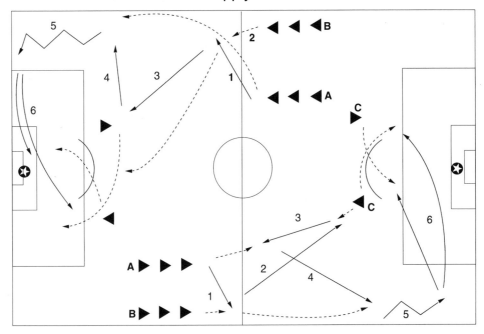

ORGANIZATION:
- Player A passes ball to player B on outside. Player B passes ball to forward C who plays combination with player A. Player A passes ball to flank for player B making a overlapping run.
- Player B crosses ball to player C and other forward making runs in box.

INSTRUCTIONS: Same drill on other side of field.

COMBINATION PLAY

COACHING POINTS:
- Pass ball to flank in front of player to maintain speed (into run).
- Cross ball one time or dribble to end-line before crossing.
- Cross ball out of reach of goalkeeper.
- Vary crosses; long, short, driven, in or outswinging, high or low.
- Eye contact between player crossing and players in front of goal.
- Players need to make crossover runs in front of goal.
- Players in front of goal need to be aggressive going for ball.
- Players in front of goal have to be in motion, not stationary.
- Make runs and passes at the correct time.
- Score.

COMBINATION PLAY 52

OBJECTIVE: Building attack from midfield over flank

NUMBER OF PLAYERS: 12-18

AREA/FIELD: Half field

TIME: 20 minutes

EQUIPMENT: 2 cones, supply of balls

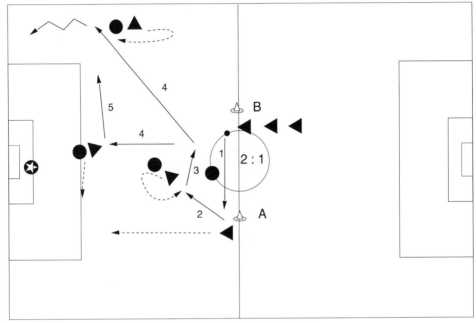

ORGANIZATION: • Player 1,2,3 play 1-2-3 combination. Player 1 receives back ball and has 2 options.
• He can play ball directly to flank to flank player (plus defender) or he can pass ball deep to forward (plus defender) who passes ball to flank. Flank player crosses ball into box to forward and overlapping midfielder.

INSTRUCTIONS: Use both flanks for drill.

VARIATIONS: Use 2 forwards plus defenders inside box.

COACHING POINTS:

- Pass ball to flank in front of player to maintain speed (into run).
- Cross ball one time or dribble to end-line before crossing.
- Cross ball out of reach of goalkeeper.
- Vary crosses; long, short, driven, in or outswinging, high or low.
- Eye contact between player crossing and players in front of goal.
- Players need to make crossover runs in front of goal.
- Players in front of goal need to be aggressive going for ball.
- Players in front of goal have to be in motion, not stationary.
- Make runs and passes at the correct time.
- Score.

COMBINATION PLAY **53**

OBJECTIVE:	Building attack from midfield over flank
NUMBER OF PLAYERS:	14-18
AREA/FIELD:	Half field
TIME:	20 minutes
EQUIPMENT:	2 cones, supply of balls

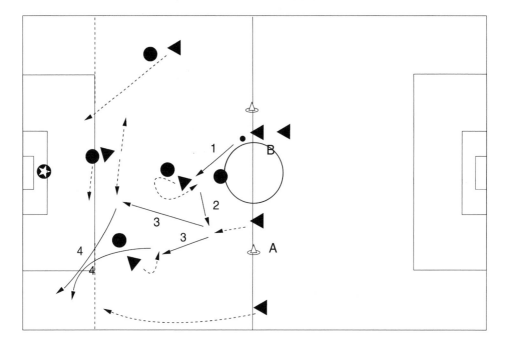

ORGANIZATION: Player B passes ball to deep midfielder who passes ball to player A. Player A has 2 options; He can pass ball to forward on flank who checks to ball and turns with it, or he can pass to forward in center of field. Both forwards will pass ball to flank for overlapping back who crosses ball into box.

INSTRUCTIONS:
- Player on opposite flank will make diagonal run into box.
- Use 2v1 situations building up to create passing options.
- Use 18 yard line as off-side line.

COACHING POINTS: Pass ball to flank in front of player to maintain speed (into run).

VARIATIONS:
- Cross ball one time or dribble to end-line before crossing.
- Cross ball out of reach of goalkeeper.
- Vary crosses; long, short, driven, in or outswinging, high or low.
- Eye contact between player crossing and players in front of goal.
- Players need to make crossover runs in front of goal.
- Players in front of goal need to be aggressive going for ball.
- Players in front of goal have to be in motion, not stationary.
- Make runs and passes at the correct time.
- Score.

COMBINATION PLAY   54

OBJECTIVE: Creating attack over flank after switching point of attack from one flank to other

NUMBER OF PLAYERS: 10-16

AREA/FIELD: Half field

TIME: 20 minutes

EQUIPMENT: Supply of balls

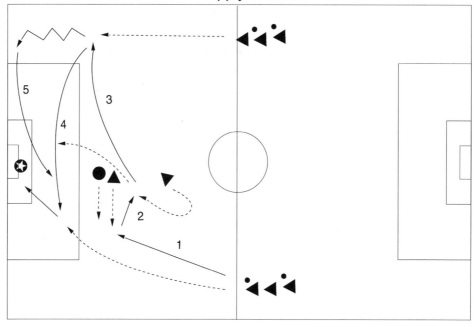

ORGANIZATION:
- Outside midfielder passes ball to forward checking to ball. Forward turns with ball and passes ball to center midfielder who passes diagonal to opposite flank.
- Outside midfielder on other side will make run and cross ball to players who have cut into the box.

INSTRUCTIONS: Switch flanks after each cross.

COACHING POINTS: Pass ball to flank in front of player to maintain speed (into run).

VARIATIONS:
- Cross ball one time or dribble to end-line before crossing.
- Cross ball out of reach of goalkeeper.
- Vary crosses; long, short, driven, in or outswinging, high or low.
- Eye contact between player crossing and players in front of goal.
- Players need to make crossover runs in front of goal.
- Players in front of goal need to be aggressive going for ball.
- Players in front of goal have to be in motion, not stationary.
- Make runs and passes at the correct time.
- Score.

COMBINATION PLAY   55

OBJECTIVE:	Building attack from midfield over flank
NUMBER OF PLAYERS:	8-16
AREA/FIELD:	Half field
TIME:	20-25 minutes
EQUIPMENT:	12 cones, supply of balls

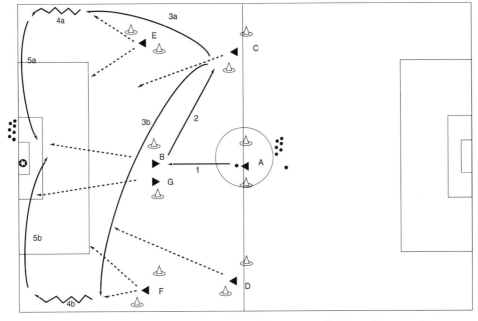

ORGANIZATION:

- Player A passes ball to forward (player B) who passes ball to player C on flank.
- Player C has 2 options: He can pass ball down the flank where player E makes a run (3a). Player E will dribble ball and cross ball from end line to 2 forwards (players B and G) or he can give a crosspass to opposite flank (3b) to player F who dribbles to endline and crosses ball to player B and G.

COMBINATION PLAY   55

INSTRUCTIONS:
- Forwards will make runs inside box plus 2 far midfielders will make runs toward goal.
- Execute drill to both side of field.

COACHING POINTS:
- Pass ball to flank in front of player to maintain speed (into run).
- Cross ball one time or dribble to end-line before crossing.
- Cross ball out of reach of goalkeeper.
- Vary crosses; long, short, driven, in or outswinging, high or low.
- Eye contact between player crossing and players in front of goal.
- Players need to make crossover runs in front of goal.
- Players in front of goal need to be aggressive going for ball.
- Players in front of goal have to be in motion, not stationary.
- Make runs and passes at the correct time.
- Score.

OBJECTIVE: Building attack from midfield over flanks

NUMBER OF PLAYERS: 16-20

AREA/FIELD: Two-thirds field

TIME: 20 minutes

EQUIPMENT: Supply of balls

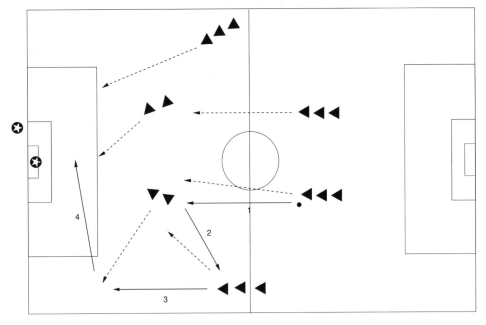

ORGANIZATION: Central midfielder passes ball to forward. Forward will play long 1-2 combination with outside midfielder and make run to flank. Forward crosses ball to second forward and outside midfielder from opposite flank.

INSTRUCTIONS:
- Have 2 or 3 players for each position for continuation of drill.
- Use both flanks for drill.

COACHING POINTS:
- Pass ball to flank in front of player to maintain speed (into run).
- Cross ball one time or dribble to end-line before crossing.
- Cross ball out of reach of goalkeeper.
- Vary crosses; long, short, driven, in or outswinging, high or low.
- Eye contact between player crossing and players in front of goal.
- Players need to make crossover runs in front of goal.
- Players in front of goal need to be aggressive going for ball.
- Players in front of goal have to be in motion, not stationary.
- Make runs and passes at the correct time.
- Score.

VARIATIONS: Introduce defenders for all positions.

OBJECTIVE: Building attack from midfield over flank

NUMBER OF PLAYERS: 16-20

AREA/FIELD: Two-thirds field

TIME: 20 minutes

EQUIPMENT: Supply of balls

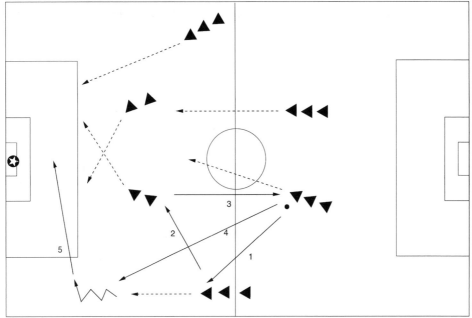

ORGANIZATION: Central midfielder passes ball to outside midfielder. Outside midfielder passes ball to forward who passes back to central midfielder. Central midfielder passes deep to overlapping outside midfielder who dribbles and crosses ball inside box.

INSTRUCTIONS:
- Two forwards make crossover runs and outside midfielder on opposite side makes diagonal run inside box.
- Have 2 or 3 players for each position for continuation of drill.

COACHING POINTS:

- Pass ball to flank in front of player to maintain speed (into run).
- Cross ball one time or dribble to end-line before crossing.
- Cross ball out of reach of goalkeeper.
- Vary crosses; long, short, driven, in or outswinging, high or low.
- Eye contact between player crossing and players in front of goal.
- Players need to make crossover runs in front of goal.
- Players in front of goal need to be aggressive going for ball.
- Players in front of goal have to be in motion, not stationary.
- Make runs and passes at the correct time.
- Score.

VARIATIONS: Introduce defenders for each position.

OBJECTIVE:	Building attack from midfield over flanks
NUMBER OF PLAYERS:	16-20
AREA/FIELD:	Two-thirds field
TIME:	20 minutes
EQUIPMENT:	Supply of balls

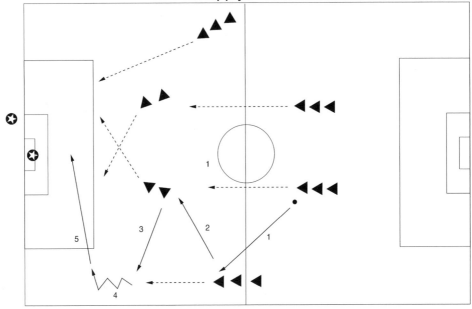

ORGANIZATION: Central midfielder passes ball to outside midfielder. Outside midfielder plays 1-2 combination with forward and makes run up flank. After receiving return pass he dribbles down flank and crosses ball into box.

INSTRUCTIONS:
- Two forwards make crossover runs and outside midfielder on opposite side makes diagonal run inside box.
- Have 2 or 3 players for each position for continuation of drill.

COACHING POINTS:
- Pass ball to flank in front of player to maintain speed (into run).
- Cross ball one time or dribble to end-line before crossing.
- Cross ball out of reach of goalkeeper.
- Vary crosses; long, short, driven, in or outswinging, high or low.
- Eye contact between player crossing and players in front of goal.
- Players need to make crossover runs in front of goal.
- Players in front of goal need to be aggressive going for ball.
- Players in front of goal have to be in motion, not stationary.
- Make runs and passes at the correct time.
- Score.

VARIATIONS: Introduce defenders for each position.

COMBINATION PLAY   59

OBJECTIVE:	Building attack over flanks from a numerical advantage in own defensive third
NUMBER OF PLAYERS:	14-18
AREA/FIELD:	Three-fourths field
TIME:	20 minutes
EQUIPMENT:	4 cones, supply of balls

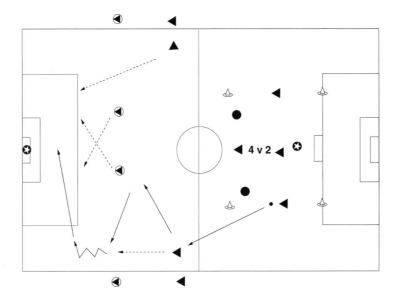

ORGANIZATION: Drill starts with a 4v2 keep away game. 4 attackers will try to keep ball in possession and pass ball when instructed to outside midfielder. When outside midfielder receives ball he will play a 1-2 combination with forward and make run up flank. Midfielder will receive pass and dribble to cross to 2 forwards and outside midfielder from opposite flank.

INSTRUCTIONS:
- Have extra players ready on flanks for continuation of drill.
- Pass from 4v2 to midfielders has to be made quickly when given signal and at correct angle and pace.

COACHING POINTS:
- Pass ball to flank in front of player to maintain speed (into run).
- Cross ball one time or dribble to end-line before crossing.
- Cross ball out of reach of goalkeeper.
- Vary crosses; long, short, driven, in or outswinging, high or low.
- Eye contact between player crossing and players in front of goal.
- Players need to make crossover runs in front of goal.
- Players in front of goal need to be aggressive going for ball.
- Players in front of goal have to be in motion, not stationary.
- Make runs and passes at the correct time.
- Score.

VARIATIONS: Introduce defenders to mark forward.

COMBINATION PLAY   60

NUMBER OF PLAYERS: 14-18

AREA/FIELD: Three-fourths field

TIME: 20 minutes

EQUIPMENT: 4 cones, supply of balls

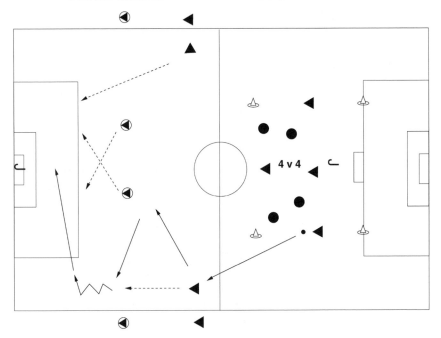

ORGANIZATION: Building attack over flanks from a 4v4 situation in own defensive third. 4 attackers will try to keep ball in possession and pass ball at correct time to outside midfielder. When outside midfielder receives ball he will play a 1-2 combination with forward and make run up flank. Midfielder will receive pass and dribble to cross to 2 forwards and outside midfielder from opposite flank.

INSTRUCTIONS: Have extra players ready on flanks for continuation of drill.

COACHING POINTS:
- Pass from 4v2 to midfielders has to be at correct time and pace.
- Pass ball to flank in front of player to maintain speed (into run).
- Cross ball one time or dribble to end-line before crossing.
- Cross ball out of reach of goalkeeper.
- Vary crosses; long, short, driven, in or outswinging, high or low.
- Eye contact between player crossing and players in front of goal.
- Players need to make crossover runs in front of goal.
- Players in front of goal need to be aggressive going for ball.
- Players in front of goal have to be in motion, not stationary.
- Make runs and passes at the correct time.
- Score.

VARIATIONS: Introduce defenders to mark forwards.

COMBINATION PLAY   61

OBJECTIVE: Building attack over flank utilizing numbers up situations in middle and final third

NUMBER OF PLAYERS: 16-20

AREA/FIELD: Three-fourths field

TIME: 20 minutes

EQUIPMENT: 4 cones, supply of balls

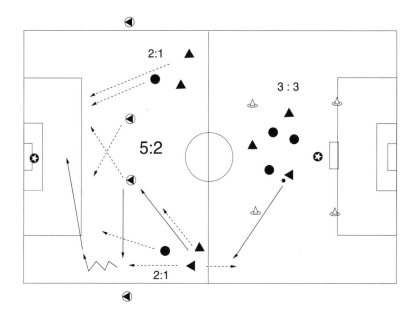

ORGANIZATION: Drill starts with 3v3 keep away game. From keep away the attackers play ball to outside midfielders who will use a 2v1 advantage to pass ball to forward for a 1-2 combination. One of midfielders will make run to receive ball on flank and crosses ball inside box where a 5v2 situation is created with forwards and midfielders.

COACHING POINTS:
- Pass ball to flank in front of player to maintain speed (into run).
- Cross ball one time or dribble to end-line before crossing.
- Cross ball out of reach of goalkeeper.
- Vary crosses; long, short, driven, in or outswinging, high or low.
- Eye contact between player crossing and players in front of goal.
- Players need to make crossover runs in front of goal.
- Players in front of goal need to be aggressive going for ball.
- Players in front of goal have to be in motion, not stationary.
- Make runs and passes at the correct time.
- Score.

COMBINATION PLAY 62

OBJECTIVE: Building attack over flank utilizing numbers up situation in middle and final third

NUMBER OF PLAYERS: 16-20

AREA/FIELD: Three-fourths field

TIME: 20 minutes

EQUIPMENT: 4 cones, supply of balls

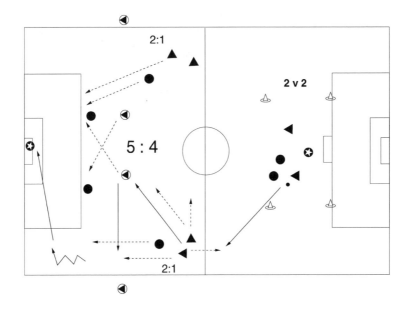

ORGANIZATION: Drill starts with 2v2 keep away game. From keep away game the attackers play ball to outside midfielders who will use a 2v1 advantage to play a 1-2 combination with forward. One of midfielders will make run up flank to receive back pass from forward and crosses ball to forwards and midfielders in and around box.

INSTRUCTIONS: Midfielder decides what kind of cross. He has different options: cross to far post, ball outside 18 yard line for shot, etc.

COACHING POINTS:
- Pass ball to flank in front of player to maintain speed (into run).
- Cross ball one time or dribble to end-line before crossing.
- Cross ball out of reach of goalkeeper.
- Vary crosses; long, short, driven, in or outswinging, high or low.
- Eye contact between player crossing and players in front of goal.
- Players need to make crossover runs in front of goal.
- Players in front of goal need to be aggressive going for ball.
- Players in front of goal have to be in motion, not stationary.
- Make runs and passes at the correct time.
- Score.

OBJECTIVE: Building attack over flank using forwards or central midfielder for combination play

NUMBER OF PLAYERS: 16-20

AREA/FIELD: Three-fourths field

TIME: 20 minutes

EQUIPMENT: 8 cones, supply of balls

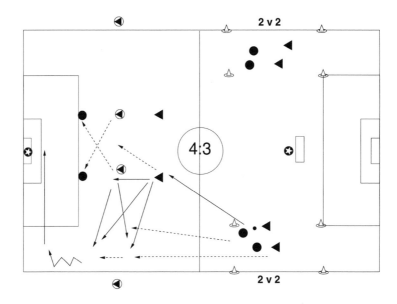

ORGANIZATION: Drill starts with 2v2 keep away game.
From keep away 2 attackers pass to
central midfielder who has 2 options;
pass ball back into run from one of
overlapping players from keep away
who dribbles ball down flank and
crosses ball to 2 forwards, or he can
pass ball to forward who will pass ball
to flank for overlapping player from
keep away who crosses ball inside
box.

COMBINATION PLAY   63

INSTRUCTIONS: Use both flanks for drill.

COACHING POINTS:
- Pass ball to flank in front of player to maintain speed (into run).
- Cross ball one time or dribble to end-line before crossing.
- Cross ball out of reach of goalkeeper.
- Vary crosses; long, short, driven, in or outswinging, high or low.
- Eye contact between player crossing and players in front of goal.
- Players need to make crossover runs in front of goal.
- Players in front of goal need to be aggressive going for ball.
- Players in front of goal have to be in motion, not stationary.
- Make runs and passes at the correct time.
- Score.

VARIATIONS: Introduce defenders inside box.

Chapter 2

SMALL SIDED GAMES

OBJECTIVE: Improving passing and supporting in game of tag

NUMBER OF PLAYERS: 15

AREA/FIELD: Circle

TIME: 10 minutes

EQUIPMENT: 10 balls

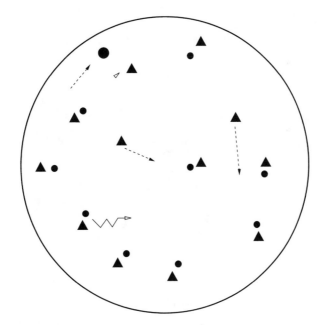

ORGANIZATION: Ten players with ball, 5 players without. 1 player without ball tries to tag players without ball. Players with ball can't be tagged. Players can pass balls to each other avoiding getting tagged.

INSTRUCTIONS: Player getting tagged will become tagger.

COACHING POINTS: • Keep everybody moving.
• Communication between players.
• Pass ball on time.

SMALL SIDED GAMES   2

OBJECTIVE: Tecnique training in stations

NUMBER OF PLAYERS: Groups of 6/7

AREA/FIELD: Full field

TIME: 5 minutes per station

EQUIPMENT: 20 cones, soccer tennis net, 4 goals, supply of balls

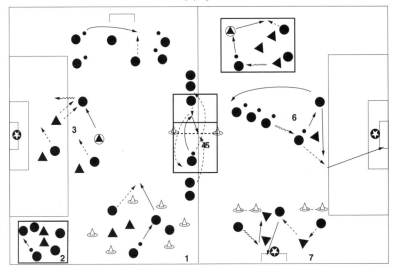

ORGANIZATION: Station 1: 4v2 0n 3 goals.
Station 2: 5v2 keep away.
Station 3: 4v3 on goal (1 neutral player).
Station 4: finishing from cross.
Station 5: 4v3 keep away (1 neutral player).
Station 6: finishing after 1-2 combination.
Station 7: 3v3 on goal (with goalkeeper) and two small goals.
Station 8: volley over net.

INSTRUCTIONS: Players stay at station for 5 minutes before rotating stations.

SMALL SIDED GAMES   3

OBJECTIVE:	Technique training in stations
NUMBER OF PLAYERS:	Groups of 4
AREA/FIELD:	Full field
TIME:	5 minutes per station
EQUIPMENT:	16 cones, 4 goals, soccer tennis net, supply of balls

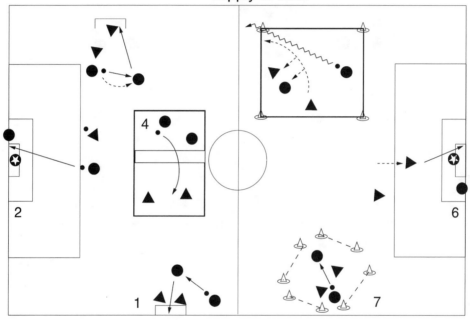

ORGANIZATION:	Station 1: scoring from cross (2 defenders).
	Station 2: shooting from 18 yards.
	Station 3: 2v1 on goal with goalkeeper.
	Station 4: soccer tennis.
	Station 5: 2v2 line soccer.
	Station 6: penalty shots.
	Station 7: 2v2 on 4 small goals.
INSTRUCTIONS:	Players stay at stations for 5 minutes before rotating stations.

SMALL SIDED GAMES   4

OBJECTIVE:	Improving 1v1
NUMBER OF PLAYERS:	8
AREA:	20 yards x 30 yards
TIME:	10-15 minutes
EQUIPMENT:	8 cones, supply of balls

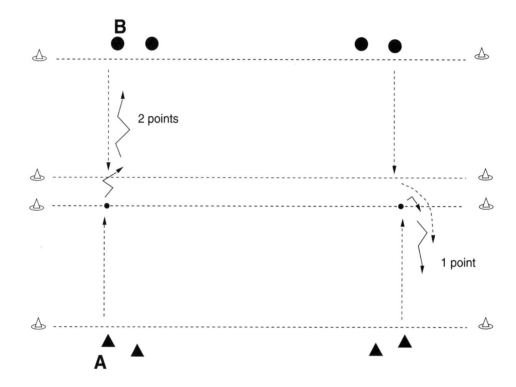

ORGANIZATION: Player A and B sprint to ball located between A and B.

Player first to ball can turn with ball and go back to starting position for 1 point or take on other player. If he beats player he scores 2 points.

OBJECTIVE:	Improving 1v1
NUMBER OF PLAYERS:	12
AREA/FIELD:	15 yards x 40 yards
TIME:	10-15
EQUIPMENT:	8 cones, supply of balls

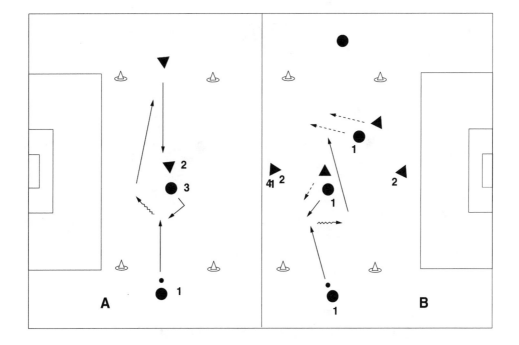

ORGANIZATION: A: Player 1 passes ball to player 3. Player 3 tries to turn and take on defender 2. Player 3 passes ball to player 4.

B: Player 1 passes ball to teammate in a 2v2 situation. Team in possession will attempt to pass to opposite side of grid/area.

INSTRUCTIONS: Drill resume on opposite side of grid.

OBJECTIVE:	Improving 1v1
NUMBER OF PLAYERS:	8
AREA/FIELD:	20 x 20
TIME:	10-15 minutes
EQUIPMENT:	6 cones, supply of balls

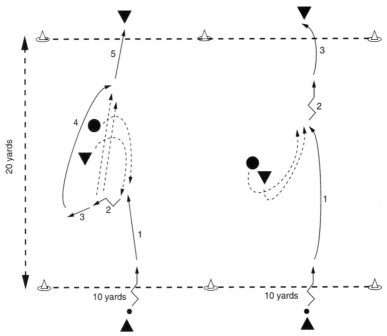

ORGANIZATION: Player on outside of grid dribbles ball toward player inside grid (Defended from behind).
Player without ball has 2 options:
1. Receive ball to feet after initial move ment away from ball. After receiving ball he takes on defender and tries to pass to teammate on opposite side of grid.
2. Player receives ball into run(on side away from defender) and passes ball to opposite side of grid.

INSTRUCTIONS: • Switch attacker/defender after each pass.
• Switch players outside of grid to inside after 4-5 minutes.

OBJECTIVE: Improving 1v1

NUMBER OF PLAYERS: 10-20

AREA/FIELD: Full field

TIME: 15 minutes

EQUIPMENT: 8 cones, supply of balls

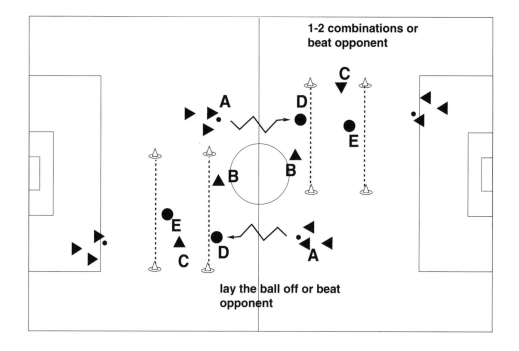

ORGANIZATION:
- Player A takes on defenders D and E defending line between cones.
- Player A has the option of using players B and C as players for a 1-2 combination.

INSTRUCTIONS:
- After player A has beaten defenders, drill starts again on opposite side.
- Switch defenders and combination players frequently.

OBJECTIVE: Improving 1v1

NUMBER OF PLAYERS: 14-18

AREA/FIELD: Half field

TIME: 20 minutes

EQUIPMENT: 8 cones, 2 goals, supply of balls

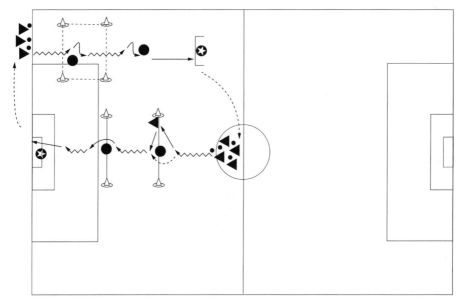

ORGANIZATION:
- Attacker takes on defenders defending line (first one with help of player in combination).
- After beating both defenders he shoots on goal from inside 18 yard box.
- At same time another attacker takes on defender inside a grid and a second defender in front of goal.
- Attacker shoots on goal after beating both defenders.

INSTRUCTIONS:
- Drill continues from one side to other.
- Switch defenders after defending 6-8 attackers.

SMALL SIDED GAMES 9

OBJECTIVE:	Improving 1v1
NUMBER OF PLAYERS:	12-18
AREA/FIELD:	15 minutes
TIME:	Half field
EQUIPMENT:	12 cones, 2 goals, supply of balls

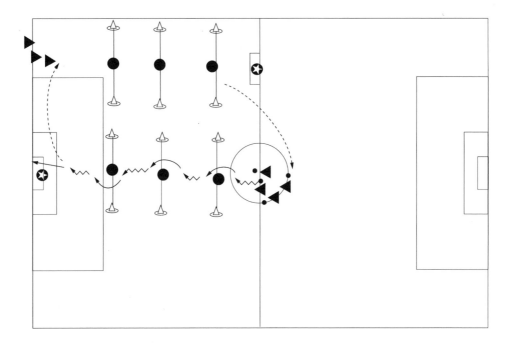

ORGANIZATION:	Player takes on 3 defenders each defending a line. After beating defenders he shoots on goal from inside 18 yard box.
INSTRUCTIONS:	• Attackers start at same time at each station.
	• Defenders can only defend their line.
	• Switch defenders after 6-8 attackers.

116

SMALL SIDED GAMES 10

OBJECTIVE:	Improving 1v1
NUMBER OF PLAYERS:	8
AREA/FIELD:	10 x 30
TIME:	10 minutes
EQUIPMENT:	8 cones, supply of balls

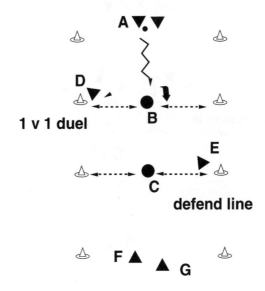

ORGANIZATION:	• Player A takes on defenders B and C defending their lines.
	• Player A has the option of going by himself or using player D and E for 1-2 combinations.
INSTRUCTIONS:	Defenders can only defend their line.

SMALL SIDED GAMES   11

OBJECTIVE:	Improving 1v1
NUMBER OF PLAYERS:	6
AREA/FIELD:	10 yards x 30 yards
TIME:	15 minutes
EQUIPMENT:	8 cones, supply of balls

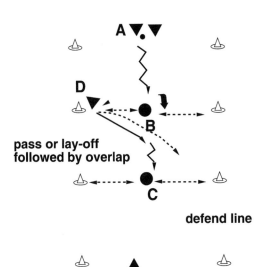

ORGANIZATION:
- Player A takes on defenders B and C defending line.
- Player A has 2 options: 1 take on defenders by himself.
- 2 Use player D in 1-2 combination.
- After 1-2 combination player D makes overlapping run.
- To support player A again in taking on defender C.

COACHING POINTS: Switch all players and positions frequently.

OBJECTIVE:	Improving 1 v 1
NUMBER OF PLAYERS:	6 per grid
AREA/FIELD:	15 yards x 15 yards
TIME:	2 minutes per 1 v 1
EQUIPMENT:	4 cones, 1 ball per grid

1 v 1 duel

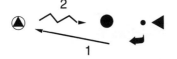

with 4 lay-off players

ORGANIZATION:	Two players play 1v1 inside grid. They can use 4 extra players on outside of grid as wall passers.
INSTRUCTIONS:	• Wall passers on outside pass back to player they received ball from. • Wall passers play 1 touch. • Switch pairs after 2 minutes.
VARIATIONS:	Player receiving ball on outside switches with player on inside and plays 1 v 1.

SMALL SIDED GAMES   13

OBJECTIVE:	Improving 1 v 1 situations
NUMBER OF PLAYERS:	6 players per grid
AREA/FIELD:	20 yards x 25 yards
TIME:	2 minutes per 1v1
EQUIPMENT:	4 cones, 4 balls per grid

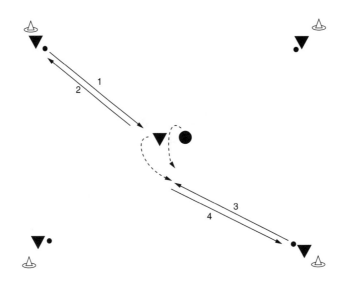

ORGANIZATION:	Four players at corners of grid. 1 v 1 inside grid.
INSTRUCTIONS:	Player at corner passes ball to player in middle under pressure of defender. Player tries to pass ball back to corner. Defender tries to win ball/ intercept pass.
VARIATIONS:	After passing ball back, player looks for new pass from different corner.

SMALL SIDED GAMES   14

OBJECTIVE:	Improving 1 v 1
NUMBER OF PLAYERS:	6 players per grid
AREA/FIELD:	20 x 25
TIME:	2 minutes per 1 v 1
EQUIPMENT:	4 cones, 1 ball per grid

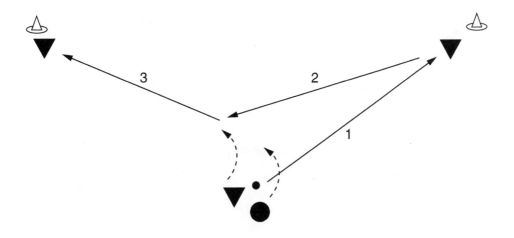

ORGANIZATION: Player in middle receives pass from player in corner and tries, under pressure of defender, to pass ball to different corner. After pass to corner drill repeats.

OBJECTIVE:	Improving 1 v 1
NUMBER OF PLAYERS:	8 players per grid
AREA/FIELD:	20 yards x 25 yards
TIME:	2 minutes per 1 v 1
EQUIPMENT:	4 cones, 4 balls per grid

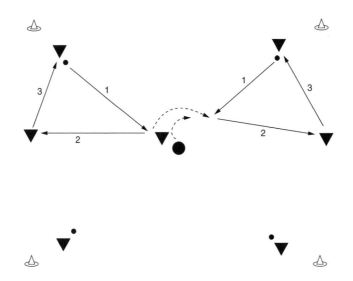

ORGANIZATION:	Four players with ball in corners, 2 players without ball between cones, 1 v 1 inside grid.
INSTRUCTIONS:	Player in corner passes ball to player in middle, who tries to pass ball to player on the side. Player in middle is pressured by defender. Players switch after 2 minutes. All players play all positions.

SMALL SIDED GAMES   16

OBJECTIVE:	Improving 1 v 1 with scoring on goal
NUMBER OF PLAYERS:	12-16
AREA/FIELD:	Full field
TIME:	10-15 minutes
EQUIPMENT:	4 cones, supply of balls

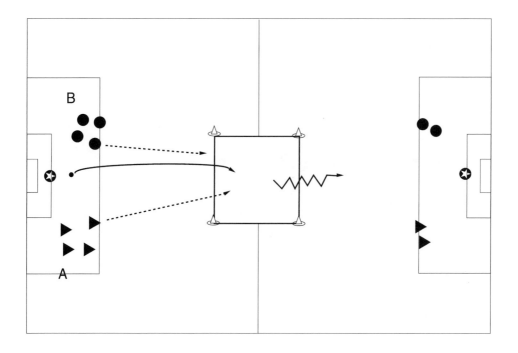

ORGANIZATION:	Goalkeeper plays a ball into a grid at midfield. Two players run after pass into grid. Player first to ball tries to beat other player and score on goal on opposite end of field. Player without ball can only defend inside grid.
INSTRUCTIONS:	Drill starts again on opposite end of field.

OBJECTIVE:	Improving 1 v 1 offense and defense
NUMBER OF PLAYERS:	7-16
AREA/FIELD:	Full field
TIME:	10 cones, 1 goal, supply of balls
EQUIPMENT:	5 minutes per station

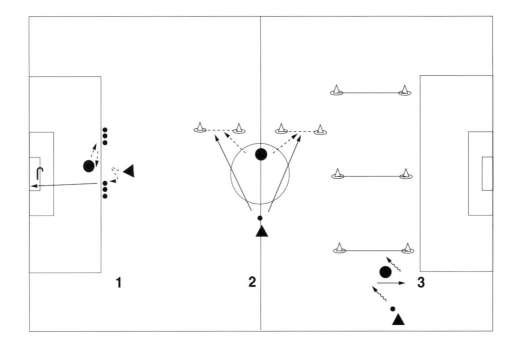

ORGANIZATION: 1. Attacker takes on defender on 18 yard line and scores on goal.
2. 1v1 on 2 goals.
3. 1v1 on 3 goals (line soccer).

INSTRUCTIONS: Switch stations every 5 minutes, switch offense-defense every 2 minutes.

SMALL SIDED GAMES   18

OBJECTIVE:	Improving fitness, shooting and 1v1 skills
NUMBER OF PLAYERS:	10-12
AREA/FIELD:	Full field
TIME:	2 minutes per drill
EQUIPMENT:	9 cones, supply of balls

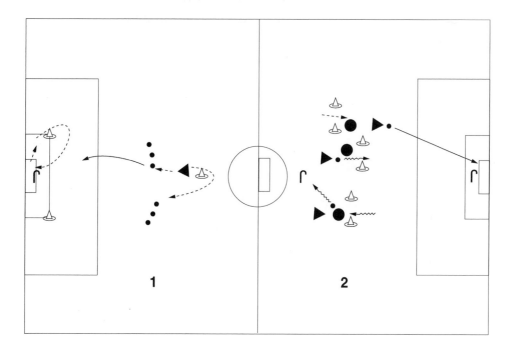

ORGANIZATION:
1. Run around cone, shot on goal, run around cone to the other side, shoot next ball. After each shot goalkeeper sprints around cone.
2. 1v1 on small goal followed by shot on goal. Coach plays ball to attacker who takes on defender. After beating defender by dribbling through small goal, shot on goal.

INSTRUCTIONS: 1. Let shooter take set number of shots before switching.
2. Work on 3 goals but don't start at same time. Wait till shot is taken before starting next one.

COACHING POINTS: All runs have to be sprints.
Constant movement.
Hard work and aggressiveness.

OBJECTIVE: Beating defender on flank in 1v1, finishing from cross

NUMBER OF PLAYERS: 12-16

AREA/FIELD: Half field

TIME: 15 minutes

EQUIPMENT: 8 cones, 2 goals, supply of balls

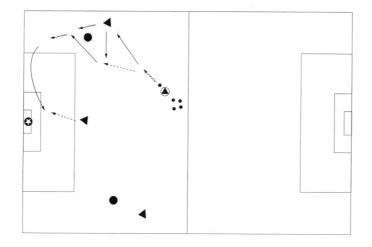

ORGANIZATION: 1v1 on flank. Attacker takes on defender. After beating defender attacker crosses ball to 2 forwards (plus 2 defenders) who finish on goal.

INSTRUCTIONS: Alternate sides and attackers.

COACHING POINTS:
- Take on defender with speed.
- After beating defender get cross off as quickly and accurately as possible.
- Cross-over runs in front of goal (near and far post).

VARIATIONS: 3v3 or 4v4 in front of goal.

SMALL SIDED GAMES   20

OBJECTIVE: Beating defender on flank in 1v1, finishing from cross

NUMBER OF PLAYERS: 12-16

AREA/FIELD: Half field

TIME: 20-30 minutes

EQUIPMENT: 8 cones, 2 goals, supply of balls

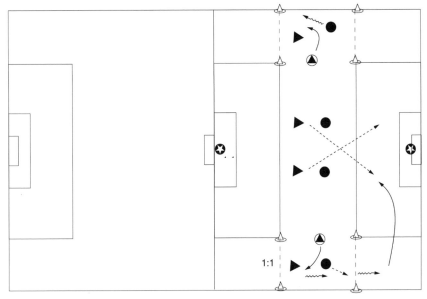

ORGANIZATION: 1v1 on flank. Attacker takes on defender. After beating defender attacker crosses ball to 2 forwards (plus 2 defenders) who finish on goal.

INSTRUCTIONS: Alternate sides and attackers.

COACHING POINTS:
• Take on defender with speed.
• After beating defender get cross off as quickly and accurately as possible.
• Crossover runs in front of goal (near and far post).

VARIATIONS: 3v3 or 4v4 in front of goal.

OBJECTIVE: Competitive small sided games with time limit

NUMBER OF PLAYERS: Groups of 4

AREA/FIELD: Half field

TIME: 5 minutes per station

EQUIPMENT: 14 cones, supply of balls

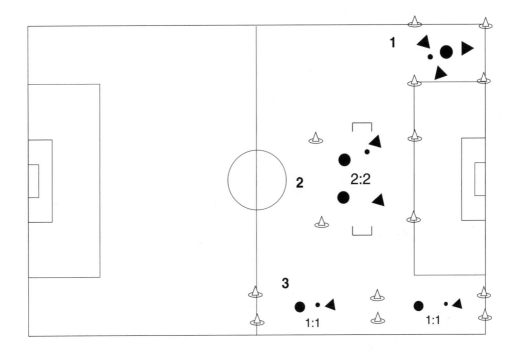

ORGANIZATION: 1. 3v1 game — each player in middle for 2 minutes count touches by defender.
2. 2v2 game — Score on small goals.
3. 1v1 game — Score on small goals — 4 minute games.

INSTRUCTIONS: Let players keep score.
Who wins tournament (all stations).

OBJECTIVE: Improving long pass and linking up

NUMBER OF PLAYERS: Groups of 4

AREA/FIELD: Distance between lines; 25-35 yards

TIME: 15 minutes

EQUIPMENT: 6 cones, supply of balls

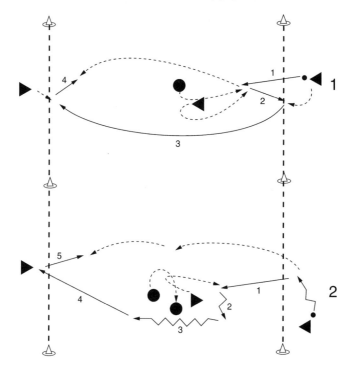

ORGANIZATION: Player 1 plays ball to player 2 (pressured by defender). Player 2 has 2 options;

1. Wall pass back to player 1 who passes long to player 3 on other side. Player 2 and defender link up to player 3.

2. Player 2 turns with ball and plays ball to player 3 while player 1 makes overlapping run to link up.

INSTRUCTIONS: Switch defenders every 3-4 minutes.

COACHING POINTS: • Link up quickly and be prepared to receive ball back while linking up (on the run).
• Accurate passing (to correct foot and correct pace).
• Communication and eye contact.

OBJECTIVE:	Practicing linking up from midfield
NUMBER OF PLAYERS:	7-14
AREA:	Full field
TIME:	15 minutes
EQUIPMENT:	4 cones, supply of balls

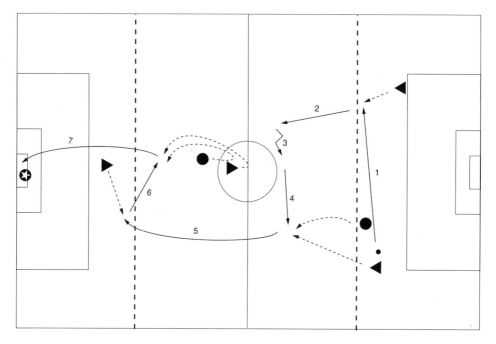

ORGANIZATION: • Game starts with a 2v1 situation. Midfielder checks to ball for pass from back and lays ball off to opposite side/flank. Player pushing up from back receives ball and plays ball deep to forward.
• Who lays ball of to midfielder who takes a shot on goal.

INSTRUCTIONS: • Defenders play full pressure.
• Game can be executed to both sides.

COACHING POINTS:
- Accurate passing.
- Correct weight on pass.
- Communication and eye contact before passing.
- Passes into run or to feet.

VARIATIONS: More defenders and attackers.

SMALL SIDED GAMES 24

OBJECTIVE: Utilizing numerical advantage situation in final third

NUMBER OF PLAYERS: 6-12

AREA/FIELD: Half field

TIME: 15 minutes

EQUIPMENT: 5 cones, supply of balls

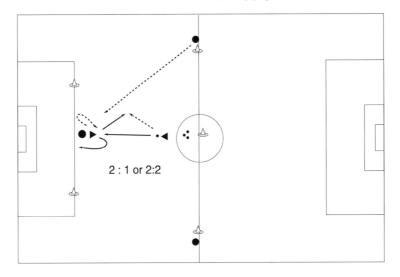

2 : 1 or 2:2

ORGANIZATION:
- Attacker plays ball to teammate who is defended from behind.
- Attackers have 2 options: 1-2 combination for a shot on goal or attacker receiving ball turns with ball and shoots on goal.

INSTRUCTIONS: A second defenders recovers as soon as first pass is made by attackers.

COACHING POINTS:
- Execute quickly, don't give second defender a chance to tackle.
- First pass has to be perfect/accurate.
- Initial movement away from attacker passing the ball.

OBJECTIVE: Utilizing numerical advantage on flanks and in front of goal

NUMBER OF PLAYERS: 14-20

AREA/FIELD: Half field

TIME: 20 minutes

EQUIPMENT: Supply of balls

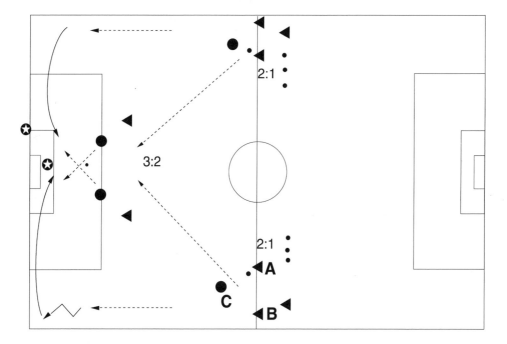

ORGANIZATION:
- Game starts with a 2v1 situation on flank in midfield. From this situation a midfielder passes ball to one of the forwards for a 1-2 combination. One of midfielders makes overlapping run to flank and receives pass from forward. Other midfielder makes run toward 18 yard box to create 3v2 situation in front of goal.
- Cross from flank to 3 attackers.

135

INSTRUCTIONS: Use drill for both flanks.

COACHING POINTS: • Look to pass to forwards quickly but at correct time.
• Forward makes initial movement away from flank to receive pass from midfield.
• Cross over runs and run to top of 18 yard line.

OBJECTIVE: Utilizing numerical advantage and linking up

NUMBER OF PLAYERS: 16

AREA/FIELD: 30 yards x 60 yards

TIME: 15 minutes

EQUIPMENT: 8 flags to make goals

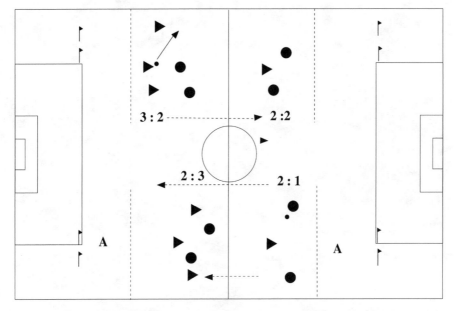

ORGANIZATION: Game starts with a 3v2 keep away. 3 attackers try to pass to attacker in opposite half and link up after pass to create a 2v2 situation to score on goal.

INSTRUCTIONS:
- If defending team wins possession they play 2v1 and try to pass ball to opposite side where a 2v3 is created on small goal.
- No dribbling in zone A (approximately 10 yard zone).

SMALL SIDED GAMES   26

COACHING POINTS: • Attacker receiving ball must lose
defender before receiving ball by
movement before pass.
• No tackling in zone A.
• Quick ball circulation in keep away.

OBJECTIVE:	Improving linking up with forwards
NUMBER OF PLAYERS:	6
AREA/FIELD:	20 yards x 40 yards
TIME:	15 minutes
EQUIPMENT:	4 cones, supply of balls

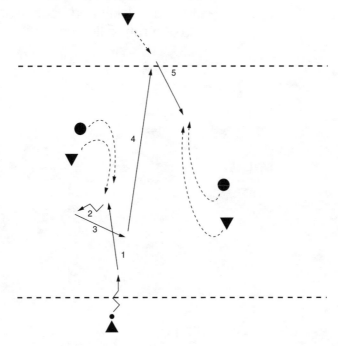

ORGANIZATION:	Game starts with a pass to midfielders. Midfielders play 2v2 and attempt to pass to forward.
INSTRUCTIONS:	• After forward receives ball he tries to pass to midfielder linking up and keeping possession. • Player that gives initial pass to midfielder can link up to create a 3v2 situation inside grid. • Defenders can score by winning ball and dribbling outside grid.

COACHING POINTS:
- Correct movement/runs and at correct time.
- Accurate passing.
- Forward has to be available to receive pass.
- Follow pass.
- Communication and eye contact.
- Link up quickly and be available while making run to link up.

OBJECTIVE: Improving urgency inside box

NUMBER OF PLAYERS: 10

AREA/FIELD: 18 yards x 30 yards

TIME: 15 minutes

EQUIPMENT: 4 cones, 2 goals, supply of balls

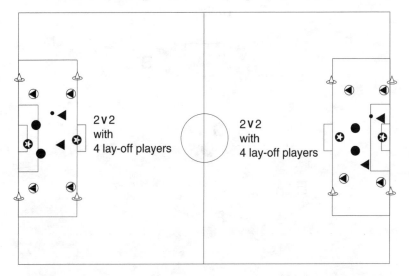

ORGANIZATION: 2v2 game with 4 lay-off players on outside. 2 goals with goalkeepers.

INSTRUCTIONS:
- Team in possession attempts to score on goal. They can use 4 lay-off players to pass to and keep possession. Lay-off players can't score.
- Both teams can score in both goals.

COACHING POINTS:
- Try to score quickly.
- Play ball quickly, correct pace and foot.
- Play direct.

VARIATIONS:
- Lay-off players only have one touch.
- 3 v 3 with 2 lay-off players.
- Score only in one goal.

OBJECTIVE:	Improving 1v1 going to goal
NUMBER OF PLAYERS:	8-14
AREA/FIELD:	25 yards x 30 yards
TIME:	15 minutes
EQUIPMENT:	4 cones, 4 flags, 2 goals, supply of balls

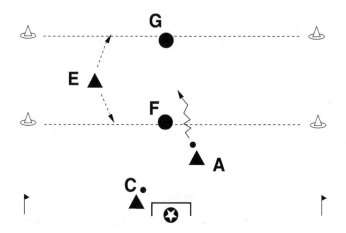

ORGANIZATION:	• Player A takes on defenders F and G with support of player E. • After beating defenders he finishes with shot on goal.
INSTRUCTIONS:	• Defenders can only defend line. • Player A has the option of going alone, without help of player E. • After player A takes shot player B starts. • Player that loses ball becomes defender.

COACHING POINTS:
- Take on defenders with speed.
- Make play unpredictable for defender (by keeping both options open).
- Defender: force attacker to side (away from Player E).
- Look to second defender after beating first quickly.
- Keep control of ball.

VARIATIONS: 2v2 game.

OBJECTIVE: Improving short combination play in confined area

NUMBER OF PLAYERS: 8-14

AREA/FIELD: 25 yards x 30 yards

TIME: 15 minutes

EQUIPMENT: 4 cones, 4 flags, 2 goals, supply of balls

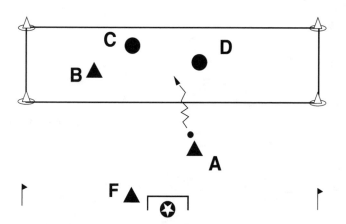

ORGANIZATION:
- Players A and B take on defenders C and D inside grid.
- After they beat defenders they can score on goal.

INSTRUCTIONS:
- Defender C and D can only defend inside grid.
- Player B stays inside grid and new player (E) starts drill to opposite side.

COACHING POINTS:
- Utilize whole space for passing combinations and possession.
- Look to go to goal, forward passing.
- Play direct or 2 touch.
- Runs behind defenders.
- Defenders: make play predictable.
- Force play to outside.
- Pressure on ball.

OBJECTIVE:	Improving short combination play in confined area
NUMBER OF PLAYERS:	8-14
AREA/FIELD:	25 yards x 30 yards
TIME:	15 minutes
EQUIPMENT:	4 cones, 4 flags, 2 goals, supply of balls

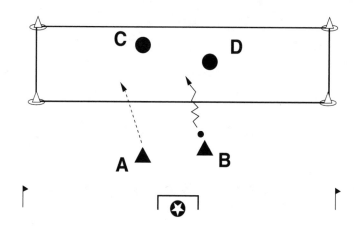

ORGANIZATION:	• Players A and B take on defenders C and D inside grid.
	• After they beat defenders they can score on goal.
INSTRUCTIONS:	Defenders C and D can only defend inside grid.
	Players A and B both start from outside of grid.

COACHING POINTS: • Utilize whole space for passing com-
binations and possession.
• Look to go to goal, forward passing.
• Play direct or 2 touch.
• Runs behind defenders.
• Defenders: make play predictable.
• Force play to outside.
• Pressure on ball.

OBJECTIVE: Improving short combination play in confined area

NUMBER OF PLAYERS: 8-14

AREA/FIELD: 25 yards x 30 yards

TIME: 15 minutes

EQUIPMENT: 4 cones, 4 flags, 2 goals, supply of balls

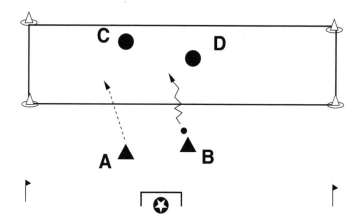

ORGANIZATION:
- Players A and B take on defenders C and D inside grid.
- After they beat defenders they can score on goal.

INSTRUCTIONS:
- Defenders can only defend inside grid.
- When defenders win ball, they switch with team that lost possession and they become attackers.

COACHING POINTS: • Utilize whole space for passing com-
binations and possession.
• Look to go to goal, forward passing.
• Play direct or 2 touch.
• Runs behind defenders.
• Defenders: make play predictable.
• Force play to outside.
• Pressure on ball.

OBJECTIVE:	Improving short combination play in confined area
NUMBER OF PLAYERS:	8-14
AREA/FIELD:	25 yards x 30 yards
TIME:	15 minutes
EQUIPMENT:	4 cones, 4 flags, 2 goals, supply of balls

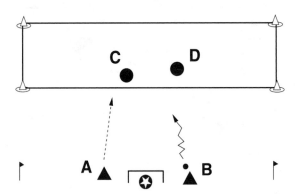

ORGANIZATION:	• Players A and B take on defenders C and D inside grid.
	• After they beat defenders they can score on goal.
INSTRUCTIONS:	• Defenders can only defend inside grid.
	• As soon as defenders win back ball they become attackers and can score on goal where attackers just came from.
	• Attackers have to switch from offense to defense quickly and defend goal.

COACHING POINTS: • Utilize whole space for passing com-
                          binations and possession.
                        • Look to go to goal, forward passing.
                        • Play direct or 2 touch.
                        • Runs behind defenders.
                        • Defenders: make play predictable.
                        • Force play to outside.
                        • Pressure on ball.

OBJECTIVE:	Learning to take on defense by dribble or combination play
NUMBER OF PLAYERS:	8
AREA/FIELD:	25 yards x 30 yards
TIME:	15 minutes
EQUIPMENT:	4 cones, 4 flags, 2 goals, supply of balls

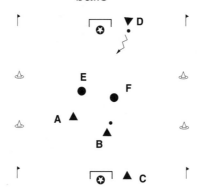

ORGANIZATION:	Player A and B take on defenders E and F. The attackers try to beat defenders and score on goal.
INSTRUCTIONS:	• E and F can only defend inside grid. • When A and B get past the middle zone, D comes out to defend the back zone. • Player that scores takes a break, other player takes on defense again.
COACHING POINTS:	• Utilize whole space for passing combinations and possession. • Look to go to goal, forward passing. • Play direct or 2 touch. • Runs behind defenders. • Defenders: make play predictable. • Force play to outside. • Pressure on ball.

OBJECTIVE: Improving flank play and positioning in front of goal after a cross

NUMBER OF PLAYERS: 14

AREA/FIELD: Two-thirds field

TIME: 15 minutes

EQUIPMENT: 2 cones, 2 goals, supply of balls

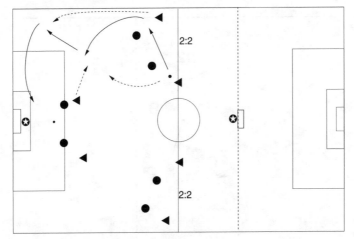

ORGANIZATION: Game starts with a 2v2 on flank. Two flank players try to pass ball to one of the forwards for a long 1-2 combination to flank. Flank player makes run down the outside to receive pass from forward and crosses ball in front of goal.

INSTRUCTIONS:
• All players involved (attackers and defenders) make runs to final third to finish or defend cross from flank.
• Start drill on opposite side after cross.

COACHING POINTS:
• Quick passes and runs.
• Movement before pass to create passing option and angle.
• When defenders win ball they can score on opposite goal; transition.

OBJECTIVE: Learning to beat a 2v2 situation and going to goal under pressure

NUMBER OF PLAYERS: 14

AREA/FIELD: 65 yards x 20 yards (3 zones 15 x 20)

TIME: 15 minutes

EQUIPMENT: 8 cones, 2 goals, supply of balls

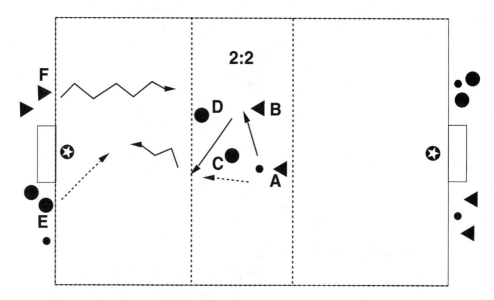

ORGANIZATION: 2v2 game inside middle grid/zone. Attackers try to beat defenders to go to goal.

INSTRUCTIONS:
• When an attacker beats the defenders he dribbles towards goal and defender E defends attacker. Attacker tries to beat E and score on goal. At same time Player F dribbles to middle grid and another 2v2 is created going the opposite way.
• Defenders can only defend inside zone.

COACHING POINTS: • Try to beat defenders as quick as possible without rushing.
  • After beating defenders, go straight to goal.
  • Shoot at earliest opportunity.

VARIATIONS: • Both attackers go to goal to create 2v1.
  • Both attackers go to goal under pressure of 2 defenders (starting from next to goal).

OBJECTIVE: Improving shooting under pressure

NUMBER OF PLAYERS: 8-12 players

AREA/FIELD: One-third field

TIME: 15 minutes

EQUIPMENT: 6 cones, supply of balls

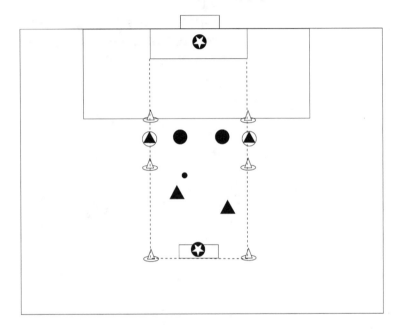

ORGANIZATION: 2v2 with 2 neutral players on side.

INSTRUCTIONS:
- Two attackers attempt to shoot on goal. They can use neutral players on side. Neutral players can only stay between 2 cones.
- Attackers can't go inside opponents' box unless to finish rebound.

COACHING POINTS:
- Quick ball movement to play defenders out of position.
- Take shots whenever possible.
- Coaching defenders by goalkeeper.

OBJECTIVE:	Improving scoring on goal/stamina
NUMBER OF PLAYERS:	10-14
AREA/FIELD:	Half field
TIME:	20 minutes
EQUIPMENT:	3 goals, supply of balls

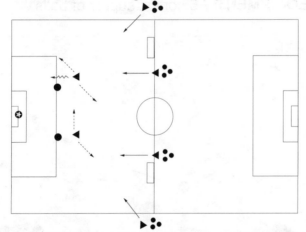

ORGANIZATION: Two attackers against 2 defenders. Attackers receive pass from various midfield positions and try to score.

INSTRUCTIONS:
• Attackers try to score on goal with goalkeeper. Defenders can score on 2 goals at midfield when they win ball. When goalkeeper wins ball, he has to throw ball to defenders.
• Let attackers receive passes from all positions before changing.

COACHING POINTS:
• Attempt to score quickly.
• Movement off or towards ball before receiving pass.
• Communication (attackers and defenders).
• Attackers must pressure defenders when they lose possession.

OBJECTIVE: Improving attacking using a neutral/extra player

NUMBER OF PLAYERS: 6 players

AREA/FIELD: 30 yards x 40 yards

TIME: 10-15 minutes

EQUIPMENT: 5 cones, supply of balls

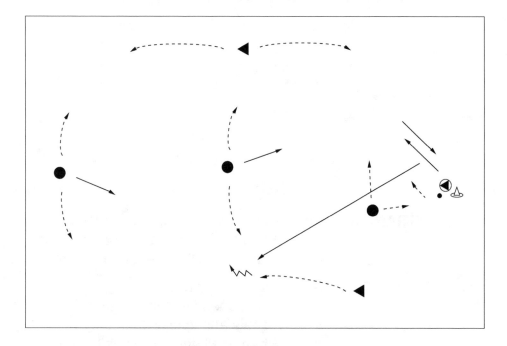

ORGANIZATION: Neutral player plays ball to 2 attackers who try to score by dribbling over line on opposite side of field. Two attackers are pressured by 2 defenders.

INSTRUCTIONS: Create 3v2 situation by using extra player in possession.

COACHING POINTS:
- Create space by movement off ball.
- Quick and accurate passing to play defenders out of position.

OBJECTIVE:	Improving creating space
NUMBER OF PLAYERS:	Groups of 6
AREA/FIELD:	Full field
TIME:	15-20 minutes
EQUIPMENT:	Supply of balls

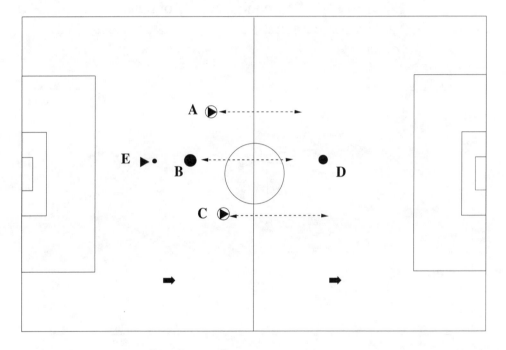

ORGANIZATION:	Players A, E, C keep away ball from defender B (3 v 1).
	Player E passes ball into run of A or C into other half of field. A and C will play 2 v 1 against D and try to cross goal line as quickly as possible.
INSTRUCTIONS:	Start 3 v 1 close to midfield.
COACHING POINTS:	• Accurate passing.
	• Passing into players' run.
	• Reach goal line as quickly as possible.

OBJECTIVE:	Improving utilizing numerical advantage situations
NUMBER OF PLAYERS:	8-12
AREA/FIELD:	Half field
TIME:	15-20 minutes
EQUIPMENT:	10 cones, supply of balls

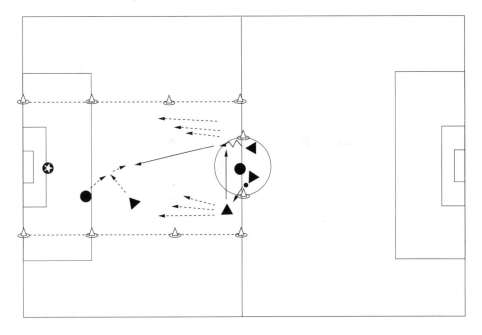

ORGANIZATION:	3v1 at midfield. Three attackers try to pass to attacker at 18 yard line and create 2 v 1 situation inside box to score on goal.
COACHING POINTS:	• Choose right moment to pass long to attacker. • Link up/support quickly. • Quick, crisp passing.
VARIATIONS:	Use 2 defenders to create 3 v 2 in front of goal.

SMALL SIDED GAMES 42

OBJECTIVE: Learning to pass to flank player from 3v2 situation to create 3 v 3 in front of goal

NUMBER OF PLAYERS: 12 players

AREA/FIELD: Two-thirds field

TIME: 20-25 minutes

EQUIPMENT: 6 cones, supply of balls

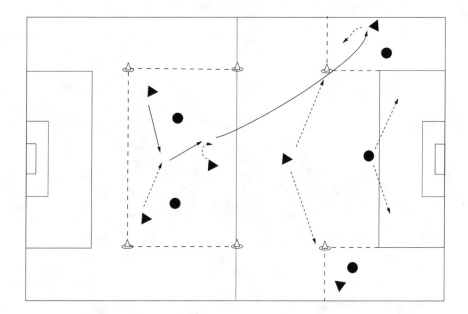

ORGANIZATION: Keep away 3 v 2 in midfield grid past midfield. Player plays long ball to flank player in zone with defender. When flank player receives ball a 3 v 3 is created. 3 attackers try to score on goal.

INSTRUCTIONS: When ball is played to flank, 1 attacker and flank player on opposite flank support and move to create scoring chances.

COACHING POINTS:
- Movement by flank player to create option for pass.
- Communication.
- Quick support in attack.
- Choose right moment to support and pass.

OBJECTIVE: Improving transition offense to defense and vice versa

NUMBER OF PLAYERS: 14

AREA/FIELD: 3 zones 20 x 15

TIME: 20 minutes

EQUIPMENT: 8 cones, 2 goals, supply of balls

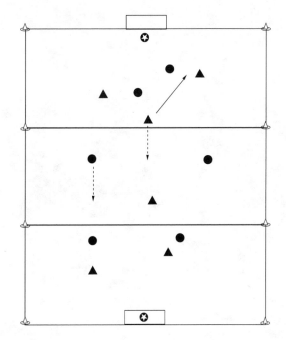

ORGANIZATION: 3 v 2 in attacking zone. Three attackers try to score on goal.

INSTRUCTIONS: When goal is scored goalkeeper restarts game by throwing ball to previous defenders. They play 2 v 2 and try to bring ball upfield to next zone where another 2 v 2 is created. Eventually the same 3 v 2 is created on opposite side of field.

SMALL SIDED GAMES 43

COACHING POINTS: • Quick ball movement.
• Intelligent movement on and off ball.
• Try to go to next zone as quick as possible.
• Keep possession.
• Attackers must pressure when they lose possession.

OBJECTIVE: Attacking from the back

NUMBER OF PLAYERS: 14

AREA: Full field

TIME: 20 minutes

EQUIPMENT: Supply of balls

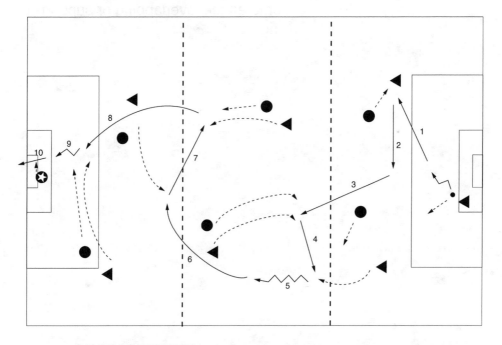

ORGANIZATION: 3 v 2 in three thirds of field to create scoring chances inside attacking third.

INSTRUCTIONS: Game starts with 3 v 2 in defensive third. Attackers try to pass to middle third and create 3 v 2 again. Eventually a 3 v 2 has to be created in the final third to score on goal. One attacker has to move up a zone each time the pass has been made to that zone.

COACHING POINTS:
- Create space/open up field. Stretch the defense.
- Accurate passing to keep possession.
- Communication and eye contact.
- Choose right time to ask for ball/to get open.
- Attacking defender moves quickly onto attack, overlapping or supporting.

OBJECTIVE: Improving short combinations and taking on defenders to score on goal

NUMBER OF PLAYERS: 8

AREA/FIELD: 20 yards x 30 yards

TIME: 30 minutes

EQUIPMENT: 4 cones, 4 flags, 2 goals, supply of balls

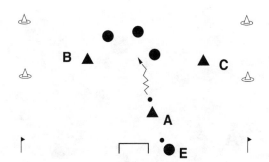

ORGANIZATION: Player A dribbles toward defenders and tries to beat them with the support of players B and C.

INSTRUCTIONS:
- Player who scores takes position of player D and D takes on defenders.
- Let attackers and defenders switch positions after set time.

COACHING POINTS:
- Players B and C get in position to support (space or passing option).
- Quick combinations or dribbling.
- Defenders: keep time and space limited.
- Stay organized.
- Communication.

OBJECTIVE: Improving short combinations and taking on defenders to score

NUMBER OF PLAYERS: 8

TIME: 15 minutes

EQUIPMENT: 4 cones, 4 flags, 2 goals, supply of balls

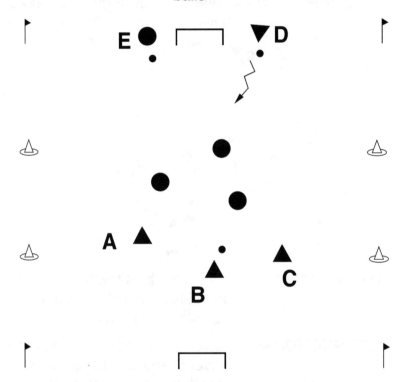

ORGANIZATION: Player D dribbles towards defenders and tries to beat them with support of players A, B and C. Attackers try to score. Defenders can score on opposite goal when they win possession.

INSTRUCTIONS: A 4 v 3 situation is created.

COACHING POINTS:

- Use numerical advantage to keep possession and create scoring chances.
- Use whole field to create space and passing options.
- Defenders: stay compact and organized.
- Defenders: try to avoid scoring chances and win ball.
- Defenders: deny penetration and forward movement.
- Attackers must pressure defenders when they lose possession.

OBJECTIVE: Improving short combinations and taking on defenders to score on goal

NUMBER OF PLAYERS: 8

TIME: 20 minutes

EQUIPMENT: 4 cones, 4 flags, 2 goals, supply of balls

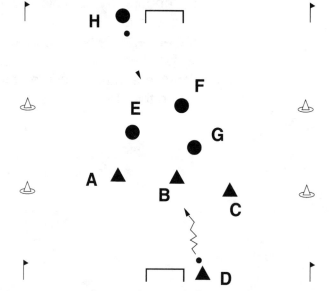

ORGANIZATION: Attackers A, B and C receive ball from D and take on defenders E, F and G. The team that scores receives a pass from player next to goal they just scored on and try to score again on opposite goal.

INSTRUCTIONS: When team scores they keep possession.

COACHING POINTS:
- Quick transition from offense to defense and vice versa.
- After scoring quick turn and attempt to score again at other end (players need to stay focused and organized).

OBJECTIVE:	Improving scoring and positional play
NUMBER OF PLAYERS:	9 plus goalkeeper
AREA/FIELD:	30 yards x 30 yards
TIME:	15 minutes
EQUIPMENT:	4 cones, 3 flags

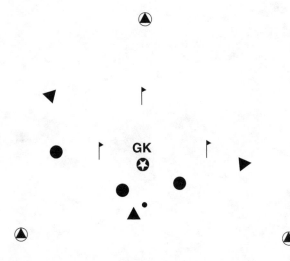

ORGANIZATION:	• 3 v 3 game on 3 goals (3-sided goal) with goalkeeper.
	• Three extra/neutral players on outside for combination/wallpass.
INSTRUCTIONS:	• Team in possession can score on goals and use players on outside for combinations.
	• A team can only score after they have made at least one pass.
	• Team that scores keeps possession.
	• Let teams switch after set time (attackers, defenders and neutral players).

COACHING POINTS: • Frequent shooting.
• Use whole field to create shooting chances and space.
• Use neutral players to create numerical advantage.

OBJECTIVE:	Improving challenges in front of goal
NUMBER OF PLAYERS:	10
AREA/FIELD:	Half field
TIME:	20 minutes
EQUIPMENT:	2 goals, supply of balls

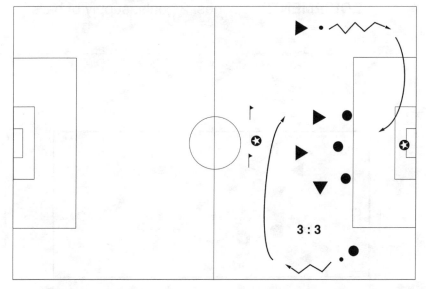

ORGANIZATION:	Two players alternate crossing the ball inside box to 3 attackers who try to score under pressure of 3 defenders.
INSTRUCTIONS:	• Defenders try to clear ball and try to score on opposite goal. • Switch sides after each cross. • Switch defenders after set time.
COACHING POINTS:	• Vary crosses; long, short, inswinging, outswinging. • Concentrate on finishing. • Correct timing of run and cross. • Connect with cross at right time.
VARIATIONS:	Play 4v4 or 5v5.

OBJECTIVE: Creating 1 v 1 situations with goalkeeper

NUMBER OF PLAYERS: 10

AREA/FIELD: 65 yards x 30 yards

TIME: 15 minutes

EQUIPMENT: 4 cones, 2 goals, supply of balls

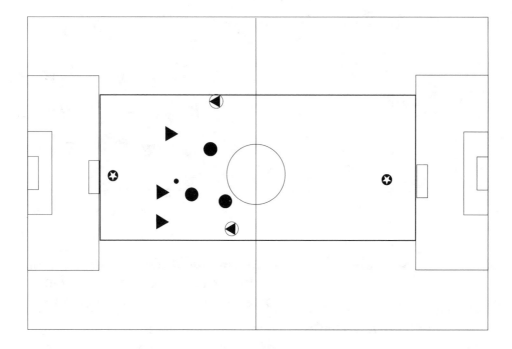

ORGANIZATION: Game of 3 v 3 with 2 neutral players.

INSTRUCTIONS:
- Defending team has to pressure attack in opponents half to create opportunity for 1v1 situations with Goalkeeper.
- Two neutral players play with team in possession.

SMALL SIDED GAMES   50

COACHING POINTS:
- Use numerical advantage to keep possession.
- Play long ball on time, correct timing on run.
- Execute as quick as possible.
- Watch off-side.

VARIATIONS:
- Play without neutral players.
- 4 v 4 or 5 v 5 game.

OBJECTIVE:	Improving fitness
NUMBER OF PLAYERS:	10
AREA/FIELD:	Two-thirds field, playing area 30 yards x 50 yards
TIME:	20 minutes
EQUIPMENT:	4 cones, supply of balls

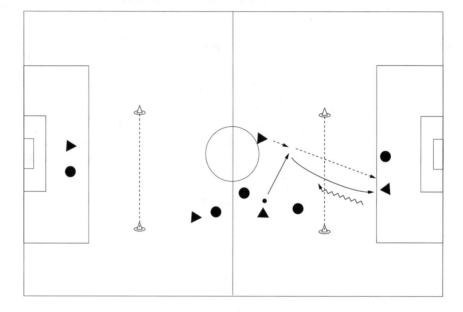

ORGANIZATION:	3v3 keep away game inside playing area. Team in possession attempts to pass ball to teammate inside 18 yard box.
INSTRUCTIONS:	• After ball has been played to teammate inside 18 yard box, player receiving ball dribbles back to playing area and player passing switches to 18 yard box.
	• Team in possession should alternate 18 yard boxes to pass to.

COACHING POINTS:
- Quick switching of positions.
- Play ball at right time to 18 yard box.
- Switch between long and short passing.
- Defender in 18 yard box should pressure attacker as pass is coming to try and intercept.

VARIATIONS:
- Vary distance and size of playing field.
- Keep score; every complete switch of position is point.

OBJECTIVE:	Improving penetrating passing
NUMBER OF PLAYERS:	10
AREA/FIELD:	110 yards x 45 yards
TIME:	20-30 minutes
EQUIPMENT:	10 cones, supply of balls

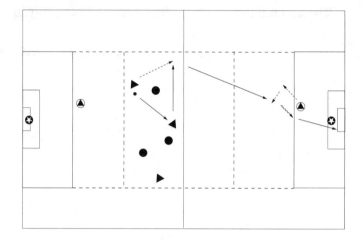

ORGANIZATION:	3 v 3 keep away game at midfield. Team in possession passes ball to forward who scores on goal.
INSTRUCTIONS:	• Team in possession plays ball after forward calls or cuts for the ball. • Defending team becomes attacking team and repeats drill to opposite side.
COACHING POINTS:	• Communication between midfielders and forward. • Forward makes initial movement to create space and passing option. • Correct timing of run and pass. • Finish on goal quickly.
VARIATIONS:	Add defender to pressure forward.

OBJECTIVE:	Improving keeping possession by utilizing extra players
NUMBER OF PLAYERS:	8-10
AREA/FIELD:	40 yards x 40 yards
TIME:	20 minutes
EQUIPMENT:	8 cones, supply of balls

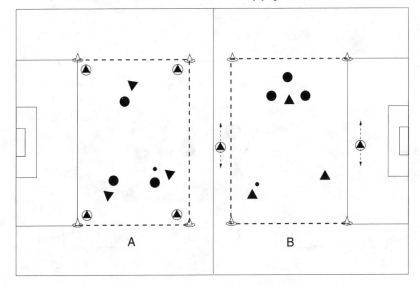

A   B

ORGANIZATION:	A: Keep away 3v3 with 4 neutral players in each corner.
	B: Keep away 3v3 with 2 neutral players on side.
INSTRUCTIONS:	A: Players are stationary in corners.
	B: Players move freely along width of the field.
	Neutral players have limited touches (1 or 2 touch).
COACHING POINTS:	• Accurate passing.
	• Movement by all players.
	• Communication.
	• Use whole field, stretch defense.

OBJECTIVE: Improving finishing skills

NUMBER OF PLAYERS: 7-9

AREA/FIELD: 18 yards box

TIME: 15 minutes

EQUIPMENT: 1 goal, 2 small goals, supply of balls

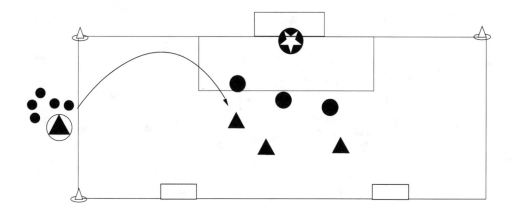

ORGANIZATION: Coach serves balls into 18 yard box. Three attackers attempt to score on goal. Three defenders can score on 2 small goals on top of 18 yard box.

INSTRUCTIONS: Switch offense and defense after set number of crosses.

COACHING POINTS:
- Finish as quick as possible.
- Movement before cross.
- Connect with crosses and move aggressively to the ball.
- If defenders win ball put immediate pressure on the ball.

OBJECTIVE:	Improving scoring skills
NUMBER OF PLAYERS:	18
AREA/FIELD:	18 yard box
TIME:	15 minutes
EQUIPMENT:	4 goals, supply of balls

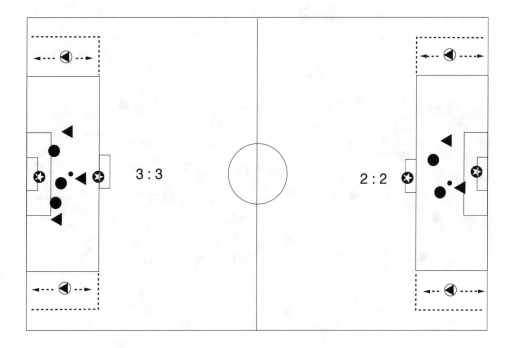

ORGANIZATION: 2 v 2 or 3 v 3 inside box. Two servers outside of box serving in cross balls. Both teams are defending 1 goal and scoring on the other goal.

COACHING POINTS:
- Vary crosses; long short, high, low, inswinging, outswinging.
- Aggressive to ball (defense and offense).
- Finish as quick as possible.

OBJECTIVE:	Transition, improving scoring from crosses
NUMBER OF PLAYERS:	10-20
AREA/FIELD:	Full field
TIME:	20 minutes
EQUIPMENT:	2 goals, 2 coerver goals, supply of balls

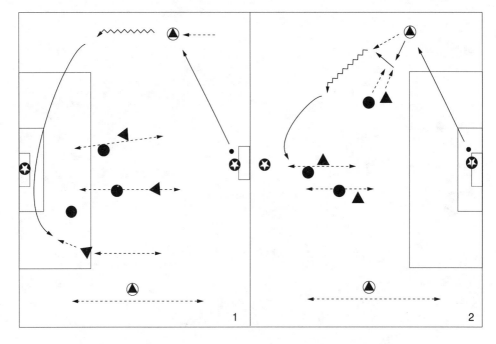

ORGANIZATION:
- 3v3 game with 2 goalkeepers and 2 neutral players on flanks.
- Goalkeeper starts game by throwing ball to neutral player.
- Neutral player combines with attacking team or dribbles to corner and crosses ball inside box. Game continues with both teams playing 3v3 until one team scores or goalkeeper gets ball.

INSTRUCTIONS: Switch players on flank after 5 minutes.

COACHING POINTS: • Play to flank as quick as possible.
• Cross over runs (near and far post).
• Quick transition (get into offensive or defensive position).

VARIATIONS: Play 4v4 or 5v5 without or without flank neutral players.

OBJECTIVE: Combination play up after long pass

NUMBER OF PLAYERS: Groups of 6

AREA/FIELD: 20 yards x 30 yards

TIME: 10-15 minutes

EQUIPMENT: 8 cones, supply of balls

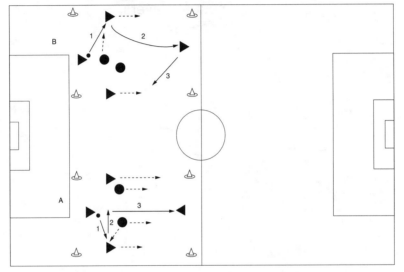

ORGANIZATION: 4 v 2 keep away game. Long ball is played by player at end (A) or by player on side of grid (B). All players move up quickly to give player receiving ball options to play ball and keep possession.

INSTRUCTIONS: Play low pressure at start of game.

COACHING POINTS: • Good passing to keep possession of the ball.
• Wait for right moment to give the long pass.
• Move up quickly to give receiving player options to pass.

VARIATIONS: Play 1 touch.

OBJECTIVE:	Movement from the back to create support
NUMBER OF PLAYERS:	10
AREA/FIELD:	2 grids of 20 yards x 40 yards
TIME:	15-20 minutes
EQUIPMENT:	8 cones, supply of balls

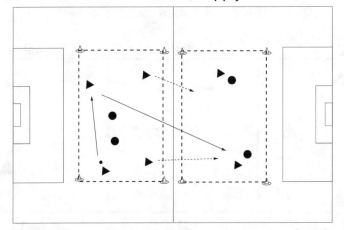

ORGANIZATION:	4 v 2 keep away game. Four attackers try to switch ball to other grid without losing possession. Two attackers and 2 defenders are positioned in other grid.
INSTRUCTIONS:	After pass to 2 attackers in other grid, 2 attackers move up to create 4 v 2 again.
COACHING POINTS:	• Two attackers in other grid need to create space and time for pass. • Communication. • Choose right moment to pass and move up. • Accurate passing. • Movement/runs into correct positions.
VARIATIONS:	Competitive game (number of passes).

OBJECTIVE:	Improving linking up between midfield and attack
NUMBER OF PLAYERS:	10 players
AREA/FIELD:	3 grids of 15 yards x 15 yards
TIME:	15-20 minutes
EQUIPMENT:	8 cones, supply of balls

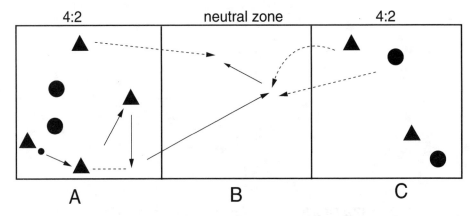

ORGANIZATION:	4 v 2 keep away in grid A. One attacker from grid C (plus defender) asks for ball. After pass to neutral zone (to attacker), 2 players from grid A link up and create 3 v 1. One attacker left in grid C moves to get open to receive pass from neutral zone and create 4 v 2 again in grid C.
INSTRUCTIONS:	Size of zones depends on ability of players.
COACHING POINTS:	• Create space to receive pass. • Organize quickly taking up positions. • Choose right moment to get open for the pass. • Accurate passing. • Communication between attackers.

SMALL SIDED GAMES 60

OBJECTIVE: Improving communication between attackers and midfielders

NUMBER OF PLAYERS: 12-16

AREA/FIELD: Half field

TIME: 30 minutes

EQUIPMENT: 4 cones, 3 goals, supply of balls

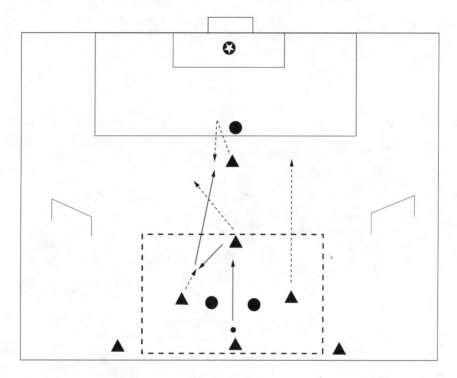

ORGANIZATION: 4 v 2 keep away game. Attacking players try to set up a 3 v 1 situation to score on goal. Player in grid (4 v 2) passes to attacker outside grid. After pass 2 players link up and create 3 v 1 and try to score on goal.

INSTRUCTIONS: If defender wins ball, he can score in one of 2 goals on side.

SMALL SIDED GAMES 60

COACHING POINTS: • Movement away from ball (grid) by attacker before receiving pass.
• Quick runs to link up by midfielders.
• Runs to create space and options by midfielders.
• Use numerical advantage to score on goal.

OBJECTIVE: Improving long passing from 4 v 2 situation with finish on goal

NUMBER OF PLAYERS: 14-18

AREA/FIELD: Full field

TIME: 20 minutes

EQUIPMENT: 4 cones, supply of balls

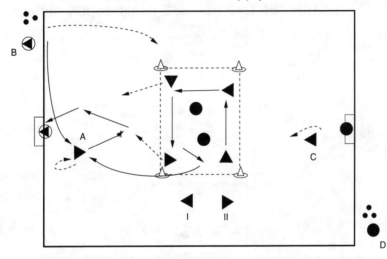

ORGANIZATION: 4 v 2 in middle of field. Pass from keep away to attacker inside 18 yard box. Attacker plays wall pass with player from grid who shoots on goal. Then, other player finishes a cross from flank.

INSTRUCTIONS: • Drill can go in both directions.
• Players finishing will become defenders. Defenders become attackers inside grid.

COACHING POINTS: • Right moment to pass and cut.
• Accurate passing.
• Quick runs to support and shoot on goal.

VARIATIONS: Add defenders in front of goal.

OBJECTIVE: Improving communication between midfielders and forwards and create attacking patterns

NUMBER OF PLAYERS: 16-20

AREA/FIELD: Half field

TIME: 20-25 minutes

EQUIPMENT: 8 cones, 3 goals, supply of balls

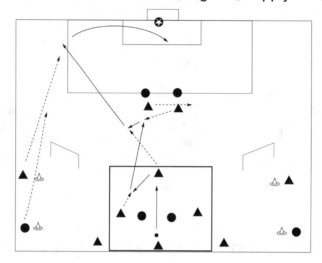

ORGANIZATION:
- 4 v 2 keep away game at midfield. 2 attackers and defenders at 18 yard box. One attacker asks for pass from midfielders. After pass midfielder links up, supports ball, and opens with a pass to flank.
- Flank player makes run and crosses ball. Four attackers try to finish cross against 2 defenders.

INSTRUCTIONS:
- Flank players are defended by defenders.
- When defenders win ball they can score on 2 goals on flank.

SMALL SIDED GAMES   62

COACHING POINTS: • Choose right moment to pass and
move to the ball.
• Accurate passing.
• Quick runs in positions to create
options and support.
• Score using numerical advantage.
• Communication.

OBJECTIVE:	Utilizing numerical advantage to create scoring chances
NUMBER OF PLAYERS:	16
AREA/FIELD:	Half field
TIME:	20 minutes
EQUIPMENT:	4 cones, supply of balls

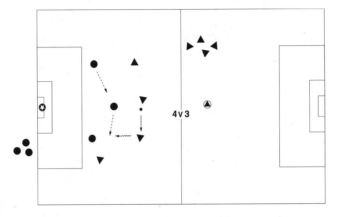

ORGANIZATION:	• Game of 4v3 in area between 18 yard box and midfield. • The 4 attackers try to keep possession and create a passing option to teammate inside 18 yard box. Attacker inside 18 yard box can score on goal.
INSTRUCTIONS:	• When defenders win ball they can score by passing to player past midfield. • Only player receiving pass is allowed in 18 yard box. • Teams change in threes and fours.
COACHING POINTS:	• Make pass and run inside 18 yard box at right time. • Correct weight on passes.

OBJECTIVE: Improving keep away in numerical advantage situation

NUMBER OF PLAYERS: 7

AREA: 35 yards x 35 yards

TIME: 15 minutes

EQUIPMENT: 4 cones, supply of balls

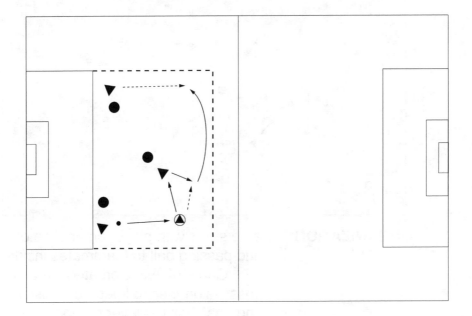

ORGANIZATION: Game of 3v3 with neutral player for team in possession of ball.

INSTRUCTIONS: Team scores points by getting 10 or more consecutive passes.

COACHING POINTS:
- Use whole area.
- Quick ball movement and movement without ball.
- Communication.
- Play ball at correct pace and correct foot.

OBJECTIVE:	Improving passing and support and keeping possession
NUMBER OF PLAYERS:	8
AREA/FIELD:	40 yards x 30 yards
TIME:	20 minutes
EQUIPMENT:	4 cones, supply of balls

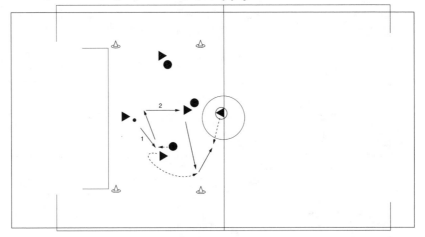

ORGANIZATION:	Game starts with player on endline of grid passing ball to teammates inside grid. Game of 4v3 is created. Team in possession tries to keep possession and pass ball to player on opposite endline.
INSTRUCTIONS:	• After pass to player on endline, team links up and game starts again. • When defenders win ball, the roles are reversed. They become attackers.
COACHING POINTS:	• Use extra players for passing options. • Stretch defense. • Look to play to opposite end as quickly as possible and support quickly.

SMALL SIDED GAMES 66

OBJECTIVE:	Improving passing and support and keeping possession
NUMBER OF PLAYERS:	8
AREA/FIELD:	40 yards x 30 yards
TIME:	20 minutes
EQUIPMENT:	4 cones, supply of balls.

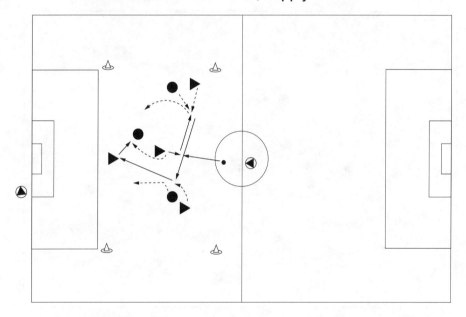

ORGANIZATION:	Game starts with player on endline of grid passing ball to teammates inside grid. Game of 4v3 is created. Team in possession tries to keep possession and pass ball to player on opposite endline.
INSTRUCTIONS:	All players play 1 touch.
COACHING POINTS:	• Use extra players for passing options. • Stretch defense. • Look to play to opposite end as quickly as possible and support quickly.

OBJECTIVE: Improving passing and support and keeping possession

NUMBER OF PLAYERS: 8

AREA/FIELD: 40 yards x 30 yards

TIME: 20 minutes

EQUIPMENT: 4 cones, supply of balls

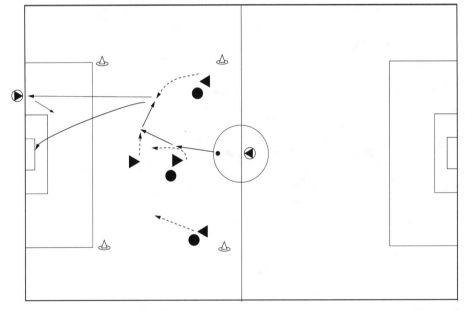

ORGANIZATION: Game starts with player on endline of grid passing ball to teammates inside grid. Game of 4v3 is created. Team in possession tries to keep possession and pass ball to player on opposite endline.

INSTRUCTIONS: • After pass to player on endline, player plays ball wide and attacker from grid links up and takes shot on goal.
• Player taking shot takes position on endline, player on endline becomes attacker inside grid.

COACHING POINTS: • Use extra players for passing options.
  • Stretch defense.
  • Look to play to opposite end as quickly as possible and support quickly.

VARIATIONS: Put a goal on either side of grid.

SMALL SIDED GAMES   68

OBJECTIVE: Learning to link up from midfield to forwards

NUMBER OF PLAYERS: 10 or 14 plus goalkeeper

AREA/FIELD: Half field

TIME: 20 minutes

EQUIPMENT: 6 cones, supply of balls

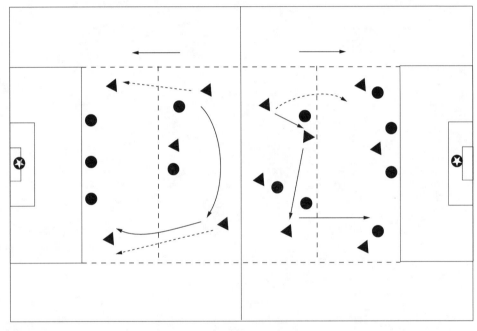

ORGANIZATION: Game of 3v2 (or 4v3) inside grid. Team in possession plays keep away and tries to pass to next grid in front of goal where a 4v3 (or 4v4) is created.

INSTRUCTIONS:
- After pass 1 (or 2) players push up and link up in attack.
- The 4 attackers try to beat the defenders to create scoring chances.
- Defenders can't defend inside 18 yard box.

COACHING POINTS: • Play possession building up.
• Quality passing to feet or into run.
• Players receiving ball check to ball at
right time.

OBJECTIVE: Improving speed of thought in keep away

NUMBER OF PLAYERS: 12 (3 teams of 4)

AREA/FIELD: 20 yards x 20 yards

TIME: 20 minutes

EQUIPMENT: 4 cones, supply of balls

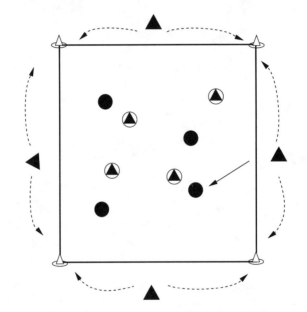

ORGANIZATION: 4v4 keep away game with 4 neutral players on outside of grid.

INSTRUCTIONS: 4 neutral players play on team in possession but can't go inside grid.

COACHING POINTS: • Play ball to feet of neutral players.
• Constant movement.
• Communication.
• Create 8v4 situation.

VARIATIONS: • Play restrictions; 1 or 2 touch.
• Change teams after set time e.g. 3 minutes.

OBJECTIVE: Improving pressuring ball as defense

NUMBER OF PLAYERS: 11

AREA/FIELD: 25 yards x 25 yards

TIME: 15 minutes

EQUIPMENT: 4 cones, supply of balls

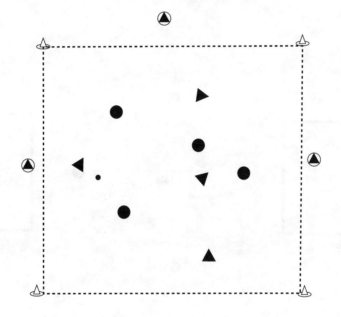

ORGANIZATION: Game of 4v4 keep away with 3 neutral players on outside of grid.

INSTRUCTIONS: 4 defenders chase ball and put constant pressure on ball to win back ball.

COACHING POINTS: • Stay compact and work as team.
• Force attack to certain direction, make play predictable.
• Constant communication.

VARIATIONS: Let teams play defense for set period of time.

OBJECTIVE: Improving positional play in 4v4 game

NUMBER OF PLAYERS: 8

AREA/FIELD: 30 yards x 20 yards (zone 5 x 5 yards)

TIME: 20 minutes

EQUIPMENT: 12 cones, supply of balls

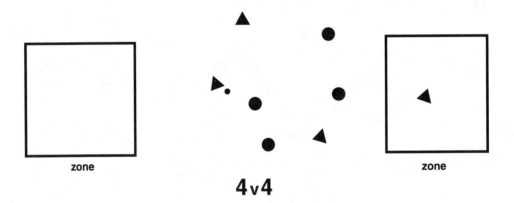

4v4

ORGANIZATION: Game of 4v4 in grid (keep away).

INSTRUCTIONS:
- Team in possession attempts to pass to player inside zone.
- Player has to move into zone to receive pass (can't be stationary).

COACHING POINTS:
- Spread the defense.
- Make runs to zone when passing option is available.

VARIATIONS: Teams score points when pass to zone is made.

OBJECTIVE: Improving flank play and positioning for crosses

NUMBER OF PLAYERS: 14

AREA/FIELD: Two-thirds field

TIME: 20 minutes

EQUIPMENT: 6 cones, 2 goals, supply of balls

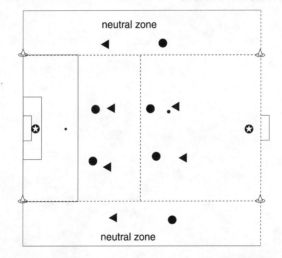

ORGANIZATION: Game of 4v4. Teams can only score off a cross from extra players in neutral zone.

INSTRUCTIONS: Two extra players on each side cross the ball inside 18 yard box after receiving pass from 4v4 game.

COACHING POINTS:
• Look to play to flank as quick as possible.
• Position in front of goal; near or far post and 18 yards front of goal. Cut to ball.

VARIATIONS:
• Open game; score from cross is 2 points.
• Extra players have restricted touches on ball.

OBJECTIVE: Improving beating defense in confined space

NUMBER OF PLAYERS: 10

AREA/FIELD: 30 yards x 45 yards, middle area 30 x 15

TIME: 20-30 minutes

EQUIPMENT: 4 cones, 4 flags, 2 goals, supply of balls

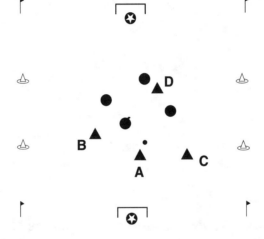

ORGANIZATION: Game of 4v4 on 2 goals.

INSTRUCTIONS:
• Defending team can only defend inside middle area.
• Play with off side rule.
• Allow sweeper to play as sweeper.

COACHING POINTS:
• Use area in front of own goal to build up.
• Use long and short passes (combinations) to beat defense.
• Runs to back of defense.
• Defense: Stay compact.
• Force attack back.
• Watch runs, communicate.

OBJECTIVE: Improving fitness, playing at high speed and transition

NUMBER OF PLAYERS: 3 groups of 4 plus 2 goalkeepers

AREA/FIELD: Two-thirds field (18 to 18 yard line)

TIME: 20 minutes

EQUIPMENT: 4 cones, 2 goals, supply of balls

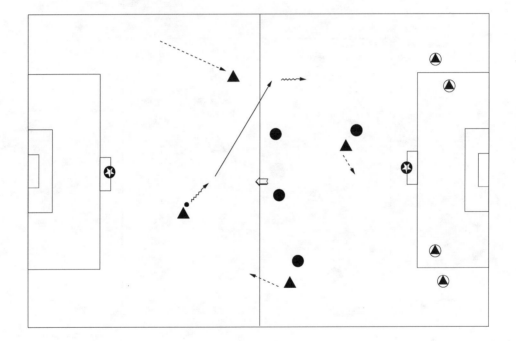

ORGANIZATION: Two teams of 4 play 4v4 on 2 goals.

INSTRUCTIONS:
- After possession is lost after shot on goal, teams switch.
- Team waiting ⬥ takes field and replaces team that lost possession.

COACHING POINTS:
- Play/pass quickly utilizing space.
- Quality shots.

OBJECTIVE:	Improving positional play
NUMBER OF PLAYERS:	8
AREA/FIELD:	20 yards x 20 yards
TIME:	10-15 minutes
EQUIPMENT:	4 cones, supply of balls

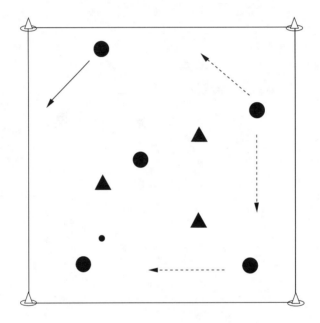

ORGANIZATION:	Keep away game of 5v3 with set defenders.
INSTRUCTIONS:	• Defenders switch after set time. • Two touch play.
COACHING POINTS:	• Quick ball circulation. • Passing on ground to feet. • Limit your touches.

OBJECTIVE: Improving 1v1 break aways from game situations

NUMBER OF PLAYERS: 10

AREA/FIELD: Field (45 yards x 50 yards)

TIME: 20 minutes

EQUIPMENT: 6 cones, 2 goals, supply of balls

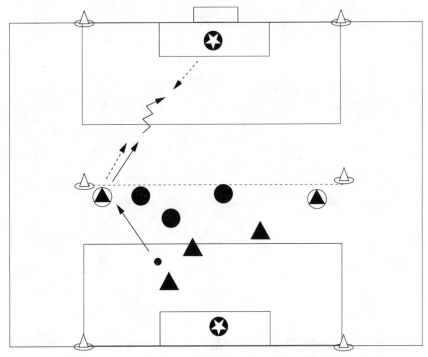

ORGANIZATION: Game of keep away 5v3 on one half of field. From keep away 1 player will go on break away with goalkeeper. Two ◓ players play for team in possession.

INSTRUCTIONS: Switch sides after each break away.

COACHING POINTS: • Wait for right time for break away.
• Quick ball circulation to set up player.

OBJECTIVE: Linking up from midfield to final third

NUMBER OF PLAYERS: 9

AREA/FIELD: Half field

TIME: 20 minutes

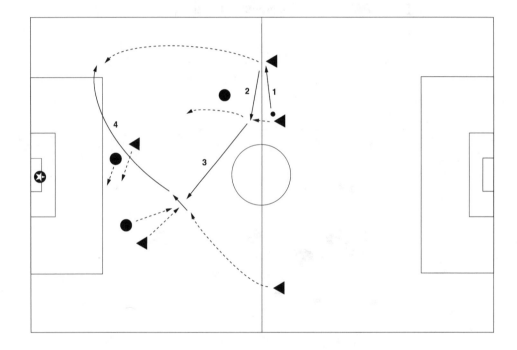

ORGANIZATION:
- Game starts with a 2v1 at midfield.
- From 2v1 player gives a long ball to forward who lays off ball to overlapping flank player on opposite flank.
- Flank player crosses ball into box.

INSTRUCTIONS:
- Start drill on both sides.
- Let players switch position.

COACHING POINTS:
- Eye contact before passing.
- Quick, timed runs to and off ball.

OBJECTIVE: Learning to utilized numerical advantage, and transition

NUMBER OF PLAYERS: 12

AREA/FIELD: 30 yards x 60 yards

TIME: 15 minutes

EQUIPMENT: 6 cones, supply of balls

± 30 yards

± 60 yards

ORGANIZATION: Game of 5v4 keep away in half of field. Five attackers try to keep possession. If defenders win ball, they play ball to opposite half as two attackers try to retain possession (2v1).

INSTRUCTIONS: When lone defender wins ball, he plays to five attackers in opposite half.

COACHING POINTS:
• Quick transition.
• When ball is won look to play to opposite half as quickly as possible.
• Quality passing to keep possession.

VARIATIONS: Play 5v4 in both halves of field.

OBJECTIVE: Improving positional play, utilizing numerical advantage and support

NUMBER OF PLAYERS: 11

AREA/FIELD: 60 yards x 70 yards

TIME: 20-30 minutes

EQUIPMENT: 2 cones, 2 goals, supply of balls

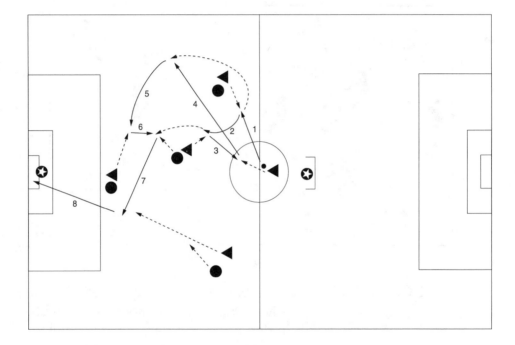

ORGANIZATION: 5v4 game on 2 goals with goalkeepers.

INSTRUCTIONS: Both teams defend a goal with a goalkeeper.

COACHING POINTS:
- Utilize numerical advantage situation to find open player.
- Play deep when available.
- Support quickly.
- Keep team shape and organization.

OBJECTIVE: Improving utilizing numerical advantage

NUMBER OF PLAYERS: 18 (3 teams of 5 and 3 neutral players)

AREA/FIELD: 25 yards x 15 yards

TIME: 15 minutes

EQUIPMENT: 7 cones, supply of balls

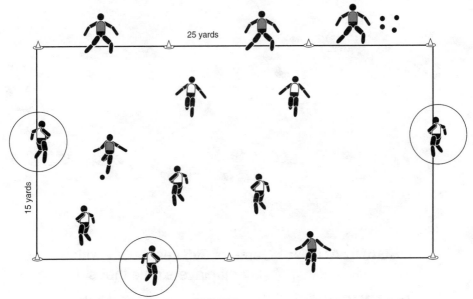

ORGANIZATION: 5v5 keep away game inside grid with 3 neutral players on outside of grid.

INSTRUCTIONS: Teams change after losing possession. Neutral players stay on outside.

COACHING POITNS:
• Keep a player in middle to act as lay-off player.
• Utilize extra players to keep possession.
• Look to split defense.
• Controlled passing.

VARIATIONS: Play restrictions on number of touches.

OBJECTIVE:	Improving long passing and support.
NUMBER OF PLAYERS:	12
AREA/FIELD:	30 yards x 55 yards
TIME:	15 minutes
EQUIPMENT:	4 cones, supply of balls

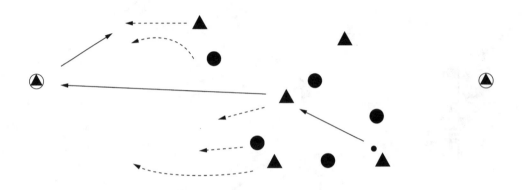

ORGANIZATION:	Game of 5v5 keep away with 2 fixed lay-off players on either side of grid.
INSTRUCTIONS:	• Teams can score point if they succesfully pass ball to lay-off player (long) and receive pass back to keep possession. • Lay-off player can't pass to player he received ball from.
COACHING POINTS:	• Look to pass to lay-off player by means of long pass. • Play at correct time (is next option available). • Support quickly. • Communication. • Keep team shape.

OBJECTIVE: Learning combination play, transition in 5v5 game

NUMBER OF PLAYERS: 15 plus 2 goalkeepers

AREA/FIELD: Full field

TIME: 20-25 minutes

EQUIPMENT: 4 cones, supply of balls

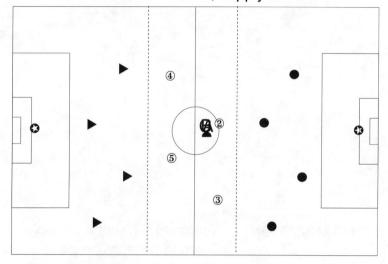

ORGANIZATION: Team A and B play 5v5 game. Team C waits turn.

INSTRUCTIONS: When team B scores they keep possession and attack against team C. When team A wins back possession, they attack team C but have to beat team B first.

COACHING POINTS: • Use neutral zone to get organization and shape to build attack.
• Utilize whole field to build attack, stretch defense.
• Quick ball movement.
• Quick transition.

OBJECTIVE:	Learning to lose opponent in keep away game, improving fitness
NUMBER OF PLAYERS:	10
AREA/FIELD:	Half field
TIME:	20 minutes
EQUIPMENT:	4 cones, 1 ball

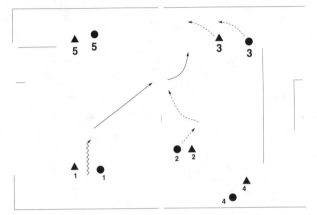

ORGANIZATION:
- Teams of 5 (numbered 1-5).
- Team in possession plays keep away. Players have to pass in order (1 to 2, 2 to 3, etc.).
- Teams are split up in pairs on defense. (Number 1 defends number 1 of other team, 2 etc.).

INSTRUCTIONS: When team loses possession roles are reversed.

COACHING POINTS:
- Constant motion to lose opponent/ defender.
- Accurate passing.
- Change of speed.
- Quick transition.
- Utilize space.
- Concentration even under fatigue.

OBJECTIVE:	Improving speed of thought, pressuring as defense
NUMBER OF PLAYERS:	10
AREA:	45 yards x 30 yards
TIME:	20 minutes
EQUIPMENT:	8 cones, supply of balls

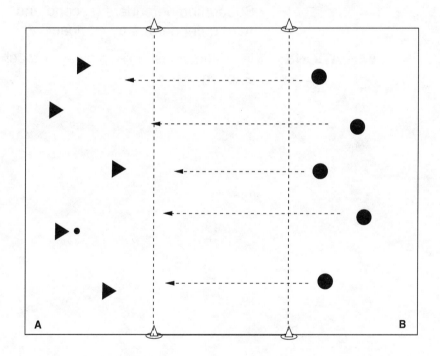

ORGANIZATION:	• Team in possession tries to cross field from zone A to zone B.
	• Defending team tries to win back ball.
INSTRUCTIONS:	• Team in possession can only use zone A to keep possession.
	• Only a player dribbling the ball can cross through neutral zone.

COACHING POINTS:
- Offense: look at kind of pressure and shape of defense before deciding to dribble.
- Keep quality possession and wait for right moment.
- Support quickly.
- Defense: put immediate pressure on ball.
- Keep shape.
- Supporting defenders (second and third defenders) stay compact.

VARIATIONS: Play restrictions in keep away, 1 touch, 2 touch.

OBJECTIVE: Improving positional play, numerical advantage situation to keep possession

NUMBER OF PLAYERS: 8, 4 groups of 2

AREA/FIELD: 12 yards x 14 yards

TIME: 10 minutes

EQUIPMENT: 4 cones, supply of balls

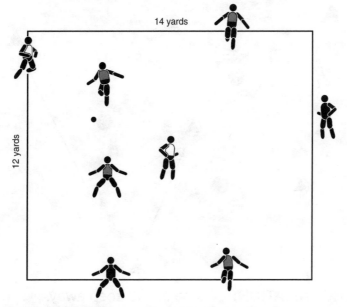

14 yards

12 yards

ORGANIZATION: Keep away game 6v2. One pair plays defense.

INSTRUCTIONS: Pair that loses possession goes inside to play defense (change as pair).

COACHING POINTS:
- Quick ball movement.
- Constant communication.
- Find open player.
- Passing at correct pace and foot.
- Keep player in middle for outlet and wallpass.

VARIATIONS: Play 1 or 2 touch.

OBJECTIVE: Improving transition and pressuring ball, fitness

NUMBER OF PLAYERS: 9

AREA/FIELD: 30 yards x 40 yards

TIME: 15 minutes

EQUIPMENT: 4 cones, 1 ball

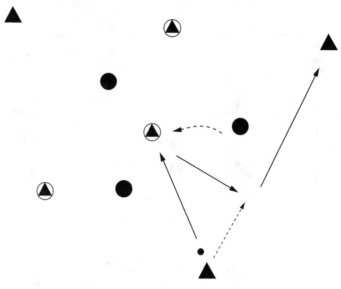

ORGANIZATION: Game of 6v3 keep away.

INSTRUCTIONS: Defending team puts constant pressure on ball (high pressure) attempting to win ball. When defenders win ball, all three change to offense.

COACHING POINTS:
- Defense keep constant pressure on ball.
- Keep shape (2nd and 3rd defender).
- Communication.
- Effort.
- Force attackers to make mistakes.
- Quick transition.

VARIATIONS: Play restrictions such as 1 or 2 touch.

OBJECTIVE:	Improving keeping possession
NUMBER OF PLAYERS:	9
AREA/FIELD:	40 yards x 60 yards
TIME:	20 minutes
EQUIPMENT:	4 cones, supply of balls

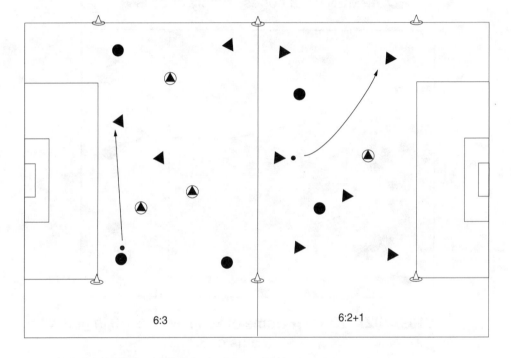

6:3   6:2+1

ORGANIZATION:	Game of 6 v 3 keep away.
INSTRUCTIONS:	Play 6 attackers against 3 defenders or 2 defenders and goalkeeper (goalkeeper can use hands to win ball).
COACHING POINTS:	• Play ball to open player. • Accurate passing. • Movement to create options and space.
VARIATIONS:	Keep score (10 passes is point).

219

OBJECTIVE: Switching point of attack and support

NUMBER OF PLAYERS: 15

AREA/FIELD: Area of 30 yards x 50 yards, grids are 10 yards x 30 yards

TIME: 20-30 minutes

EQUIPMENT: 8 cones, supply of balls

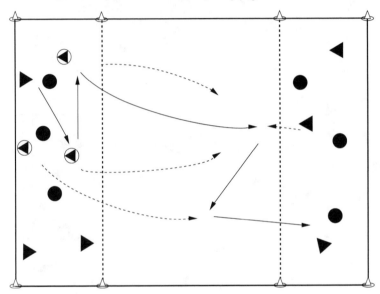

ORGANIZATION:
- Game of keep away 6 v 3 in grid with 3 teams of 3.
- Player passes ball to other side of area and 3 players move to support to create 6 v 3 in other grid.

INSTRUCTIONS: Team of player that makes pass will link up to other side for new 6 v 3.

COACHING POINTS:
- Pass at right time (player receiving needs to create option).
- Link up as quickly as possible.
- Create passing options while linking up.

OBJECTIVE: Improving utilizing numerical superiority in limited space

NUMBER OF PLAYERS: 9

AREA/FIELD: 15 yards x 20 yards

TIME: 15 minutes

EQUIPMENT: 4 cones, supply of balls

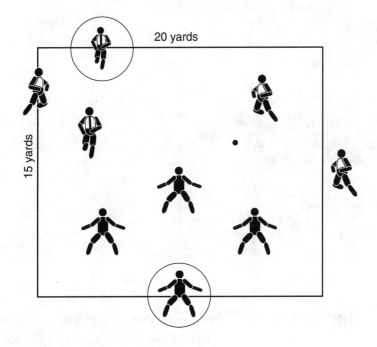

20 yards

15 yards

ORGANIZATION: 3 v 3 keep away with 3 neutral players.

INSTRUCTIONS: Three neutral players can move around freely outside grid.

COACHING POINTS:
• Accurate passing.
• Use neutral players for extra passing options.
• Quick, short movement.

SMALL SIDED GAMES 90

OBJECTIVE: Creating scoring chances from build up in midfield

NUMBER OF PLAYERS: 11

AREA/FIELD: 50 yards x 60 yards

TIME: 20 minutes

EQUIPMENT: 9 cones, supply of balls

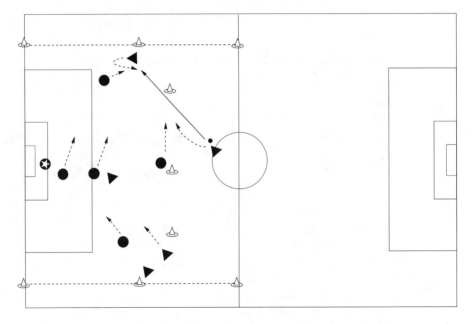

ORGANIZATION: Team in possession plays ball around until they find opening to create shot or cross.

INSTRUCTIONS:
• Defending team can only defend up to cones.
• When defenders win ball they can score by dribbling through cones.

COACHING POINTS:
• Use neutral zone to set up final pass or penetrating pass.
• Quick ball movement to stretch and disorganize defense.

OBJECTIVE:	Support after long pass into final third of field
NUMBER OF PLAYERS:	12
AREA/FIELD:	Two-thirds field
TIME:	20 minutes
EQUIPMENT:	Supply of balls

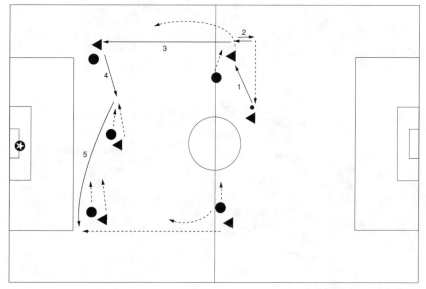

ORGANIZATION: Game of 6v5 on goal with goalkeeper.

INSTRUCTIONS: Attacking team uses numerical advantage to keep possession of ball and to create long pass opportunities.

COACHING POINTS:
- Attacking team needs to utilize whole playing area to stretch defense and to create space.
- Movement to and away from ball to create passing options.
- Play ball deep on time.
- Support quickly after long pass, creating passing or crossing options.
- Create scoring chances.

OBJECTIVE:	Improving long pass to forward in advanced position (final pass)
NUMBER OF PLAYERS:	15
AREA/FIELD:	Full field
TIME:	20 minutes
EQUIPMENT:	6 cones, supply of balls

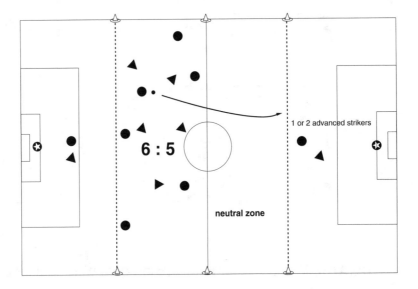

ORGANIZATION:	• Keep away game of 6 v 5 in neutral zone.
	• Team in possession tries to play long ball deep to forward.
	• Forward tries to score under pressure of defender.
INSTRUCTIONS:	• After pass to forward team switch to other neutral zone to create another 6v5.
	• Attack other goal.

COACHING POINTS:
- Play long ball at right time.
- Forward decides when ball is played (eye contact and communication).
- Create a passing opportunity by quick ball movement and movement by players.

VARIATIONS:
- Let 1 player link up with forward to create 2v1 in front of goal.
- Two deep forwards with defenders.

SMALL SIDED GAMES 93

OBJECTIVE: Improving linking up after long pass

NUMBER OF PLAYERS: 13

AREA/FIELD: 2 grids of 30 yards x 30 yards, 10 yards apart

TIME: 15 minutes

EQUIPMENT: 8 cones, supply of balls

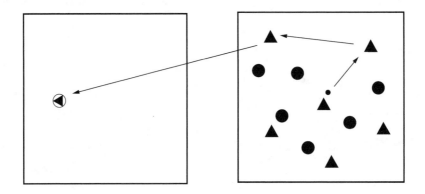

ORGANIZATION: Two teams play keep away 6 v 6 inside grid. Team in possession will attempt to pass long to player in opposite grid.

INSTRUCTIONS:
- After pass, 5 players of attacking team and all 6 defenders sprint to other grid to link up.
- Team in possession plays keep away and attempts to play long ball again to other grid.

COACHING POINTS:
- Play ball to moving player.
- Link up as quickly as possible.
- While linking up, get into position to receive ball and keep possession.
- Play ball at right time.

SMALL SIDED GAMES   94

OBJECTIVE: Utilizing flanks to create scoring chances from crosses

NUMBER OF PLAYERS: 14

AREA/FIELD: Half field

TIME: 20 minutes

EQUIPMENT: 8 cones, 2 goals, supply of balls

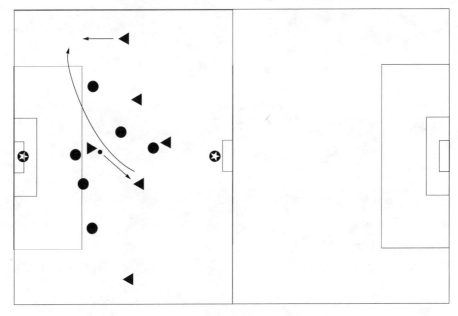

ORGANIZATION: Team in possession plays 4 v 6 with 2 teammates in neutral zones on flank.

INSTRUCTIONS:
- Attackers try to pass to teammate on flank as soon as possible.
- Player on flank will receive ball and cross ball to teammates in front of goal.
- No defenders in neutral zone.
- When defense wins ball, or after goal has been scored game continues as defenders attack other goal 4v4.

227

COACHING POINTS:
- When ball is passed to right flank, player on left flank will pinch to inside.
- Cross out of reach of goalkeeper.
- Crossover runs to confuse defense.
- Aggressive movement to ball (offense and defense).

OBJECTIVE: Creating scoring chances

NUMBER OF PLAYERS: 13 (Including goalkeeper)

AREA/FIELD: 55 yards x 55 yards

TIME: 20 minutes

EQUIPMENT: 6 cones, supply of balls

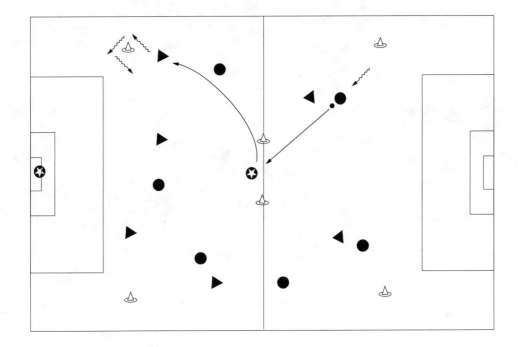

ORGANIZATION:
- Two teams play 6v6 inside playing area.
- Both teams can score on goal in middle.

INSTRUCTIONS:
- Goals can be scored from both sides of goal (with goalkeeper).
- After teams score or team wins back ball, they have to dribble around one of outside cones.

COACHING POINTS: • Look to score quickly.
• Switch point of attack using whole field.
• Be creative taking on players or creating scoring chances.

OBJECTIVE: Creating scoring chances

NUMBER OF PLAYERS: 14

AREA/FIELD: 50 yards x 70 yards

TIME: 20 minutes

EQUIPMENT: 4 cones, 2 goals, supply of balls

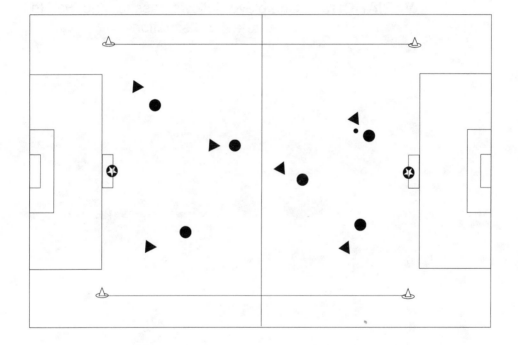

ORGANIZATION: 3 v 3 game attacking goal with goal-keeper played in 2 halves.

INSTRUCTIONS:
- Game starts with 3v3 on goal. When defense wins back ball or when attackers score, defenders will attempt to pass ball to other side to teammates who then play another 3v3 on other side of field.
- No players can cross half way line.

COACHING POINTS:
- Create scoring chances as quickly as possible.
- Quick movement on and off ball.
- When ball is won on defense, find teammates on other side as quickly as possible (without losing possession).

VARIATIONS: One player follows pass to other half to create a 4 v 3 situation.

OBJECTIVE:	Improving building over flanks by utilizing numerical advantage
NUMBER OF PLAYERS:	14
AREA/FIELD:	70 yards x 45 yards
TIME:	30 minutes
EQUIPMENT:	2 cones, 2 goals, supply of balls

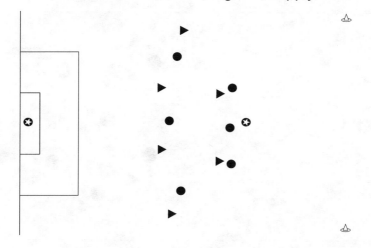

ORGANIZATION:	Game of 6 v 6 plus 2 goalkeepers.
INSTRUCTIONS:	• Team A plays 4:2 formation. • Team B plays 3:3 formation.
COACHING POINTS:	**Team A:** Utilize numerical advantage (4 against 3) when building up. • Use width of field. • Quick ball movement to create passing options. • Forwards check back to ball. **Team B:** Slide and shift to create numbers around ball. • Communication. • Force offense to play difficult passes and try to win ball.

OBJECTIVE:	Defending (stopping) long pass
NUMBER OF PLAYERS:	14
AREA/FIELD:	20 yards x 50 yards
TIME:	20-30 minutes
EQUIPMENT:	6 cones, supply of balls

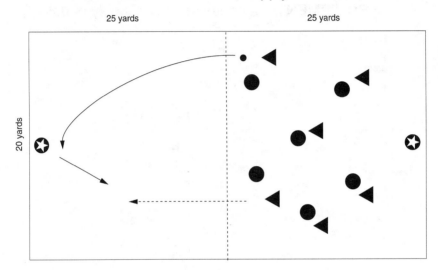

ORGANIZATION:	Game of 6 v 6 in half of field. Two goalkeepers on either side of field.
INSTRUCTIONS:	Team in possession will try to play keep away and attempt to pass ball to goalkeeper on other side of the field. Defending team will try to win ball and stop team in possession playing long ball to other goalkeeper.
COACHING POINTS:	• Pressure ball. • Force players in possession to side or back (facing own goalkeeper). • All players must be organized and disciplined in marking. • Communication.

VARIATIONS: Instead of passing the to the goalkeepers, add two goals and let teams
shoot and score on the goalkeepers.

OBJECTIVE:	Improving keeping possession
NUMBER OF PLAYERS:	9
AREA/FIELD:	25 yards x 25 yards
TIME:	15 minutes
EQUIPMENT:	4 cones, supply of balls

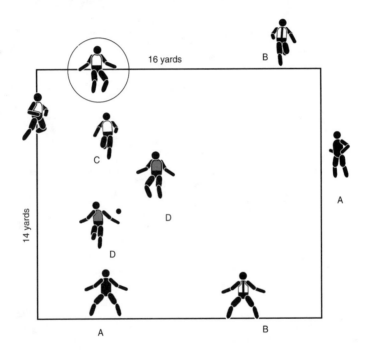

ORGANIZATION: 7 v 2 keep away game.

INSTRUCTIONS:
- Four pairs with 1 extra player.
- Seven players play keep away. When possession is lost, pair that lost ball will go in middle to defend.
- Play 2 touch.

COACHING POINTS: Utilize whole grid space.
Communication.

SMALL SIDED GAMES 100

OBJECTIVE: Improving positional play

NUMBER OF PLAYERS: 12

AREA/FIELD: Center circle

TIME: 15 minutes

EQUIPMENT: Supply of balls

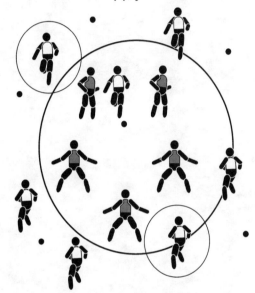

ORGANIZATION: Team in possession plays a 7 v 5 keep away game (5 plus 2 extra players on outside).

INSTRUCTIONS:
- Four players plus 2 extra players on outside of grid, 1 player in middle.
- The 7 players try to keep possession of ball by passing. Five defenders can only stay inside circle and try to win back ball. As soon as defending team wins ball they change to outside and play keep away (1 player stays in middle).
- Team that lost possession will defend inside grid.

SMALL SIDED GAMES 100

COACHING POINTS: • Quick transition when ball is lost or won (quick change of positions).
• Try to split defenders (passes to player in middle).
• Keep ball on ground and play to feet.

SMALL SIDED GAMES 101

OBJECTIVE:	Attacking from the back
NUMBER OF PLAYERS:	16
AREA/FIELD:	Three-fourths field
TIME:	30 minutes
EQUIPMENT:	4 cones, 2 goals, supply of balls

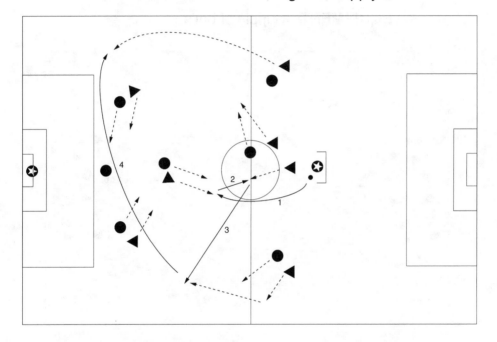

ORGANIZATION:	Game of 7v7 with 2 goalkeepers.
INSTRUCTIONS:	• Defending team plays 4:2:1 formation.
	• Attacking team plays 3:1:3 formation.
COACHING POINTS:	• Look to make forward runs overlaps and to play long balls on time.
	• Create space for long ball and runs by letting other players make runs away from that space.
	• Start run on time, pass on time.
	• Communication.

SMALL SIDED GAMES 102

OBJECTIVE: Utilizing numerical advantage to keep possession

NUMBER OF PLAYERS: 10

AREA/FIELD: 18 yard box

TIME: 10-15 minutes

EQUIPMENT: Supply of balls

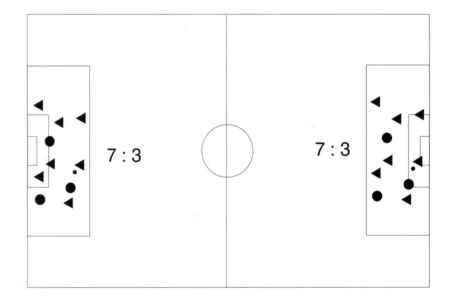

ORGANIZATION: 7 v 3 keep away inside penalty box.

INSTRUCTIONS:
• 10 consecutive passes scores a point.
• Play 2 touch maximum.

COACHING POINTS:
• Numbers around ball as well as numbers away from ball.
• Use whole playing area.
• Quick ball movement away from defenders.

VARIATIONS: Add goalkeeper and try to score on goal.

OBJECTIVE: Creating shooting chances outside 18 yard box

NUMBER OF PLAYERS: 16

AREA/FIELD: 40 yards x 36 yards

TIME: 20 minutes

EQUIPMENT: 4 cones, 2 goals, supply of balls

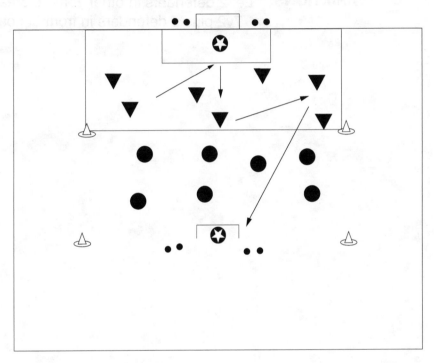

ORGANIZATION: Two teams of 7 players pass ball around in own zone (no defenders in their zone) and shoot on goal.

INSTRUCTIONS:
- Team in possession plays ball around until a shooting chance has been created.
- Team in possession only has 5 passes to create scoring chance.

SMALL SIDED GAMES 103

COACHING POINTS:
- Spread out on offense, stretch defense.
- Set up quality shots by accurate passing.
- Passing has to be quick to disorganize defense.
- Defenders cut off shooting angles.

VARIATIONS: Let 2 defenders in other zone to create 7v2 plus 5 defenders in front of goal.

SMALL SIDED GAMES 104

OBJECTIVE:	Shooting from outside 18 yard box after lay-off pass
NUMBER OF PLAYERS:	16
AREA:	40 yards x 36 yards
TIME:	15 minutes
EQUIPMENT:	4 cones, 2 goals, supply of balls

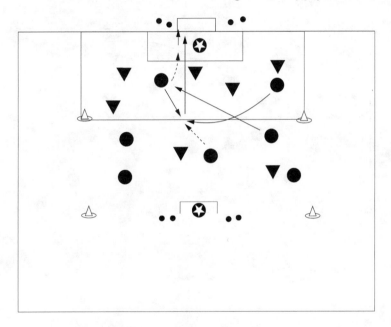

ORGANIZATION:	5 v 2 keep away with 2 forwards inside 18 yard box.
INSTRUCTIONS:	Five attackers play keep away and play ball to forward. Forward play ball back to outside 18 to teammate who shoots on goal.
COACHING POINTS:	• Quick ball movement. • Look for forward quickly. • Play ball accurately. • Forward follows shot for rebound.

SMALL SIDED GAMES 105

OBJECTIVE: Creating scoring chances from crosses

NUMBER OF PLAYERS: 16

AREA/FIELD: 70 yards x 36 yards

TIME: 15 minutes

EQUIPMENT: 12 cones, 2 goals, supply of balls

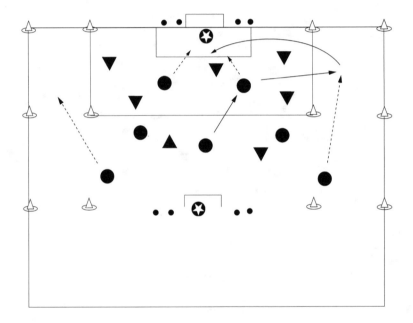

ORGANIZATION: 5 v 2 keep away in own half plus 2 forwards in other half.

INSTRUCTIONS: Five attackers play keep away against 2 defenders. They attempt to pass ball to forward for a combination to flank. One of attackers makes run to neutral zone to receive pass from forward and crosses ball inside box where 2 forwards try to score.

SMALL SIDED GAMES 105

COACHING POINTS:
- Quick, accurate ball movement by attackers.
- Find attacker as soon as possible.
- Forwards make crossover runs in front of goal.
- Pass and make runs at correct time.

SMALL SIDED GAMES 106

OBJECTIVE: Improving attacking and creating scoring chances by attacking over flank

NUMBER OF PLAYERS: 16

AREA/FIELD: 70 yards x 36 yards

TIME: 20 minutes

EQUIPMENT: 12 cones, 2 goals, supply of balls

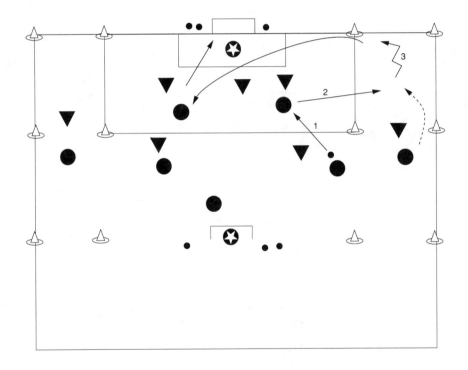

ORGANIZATION: Game of 7 v 7 with neutral zones on both flanks.

INSTRUCTIONS:
- Team in possession plays keep away until they find opportunity to play ball into neutral zone.
- No defenders in neutral zone.

SMALL SIDED GAMES 106

COACHING POINTS:
- Look to play to flank quickly.
- Create passing options by movement to and away from ball.
- Cross to teammates in front of goal.
- Crossover runs.
- Blind side runs.
- Balance between players going forward and players staying back.

SMALL SIDED GAMES 107

OBJECTIVE: Improving communication and taking over positions (tactically)

NUMBER OF PLAYERS: 10

AREA/FIELD: 30 yards x 20 yards

TIME: 15 minutes

EQUIPMENT: 8 cones, supply of balls

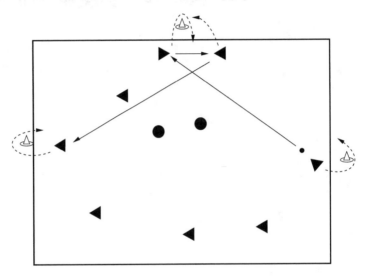

ORGANIZATION: Keep away game 8 v 2 in grid. 4 cones are place outside grid.

INSTRUCTIONS: After player has passed ball he sprints around one of the cones on outside of grid. After sprint he returns to keep away game.

COACHING POINTS:
- Quick movement after pass.
- Return to grid looking for new position (where are you needed).
- Other attackers move to support positions.
- Communication.

SMALL SIDED GAMES 108

OBJECTIVE:	Improving positional play in 8 v 7 game
NUMBER OF PLAYERS:	15
AREA/FIELD:	Half field
TIME:	20 minutes
EQUIPMENT:	Supply of balls

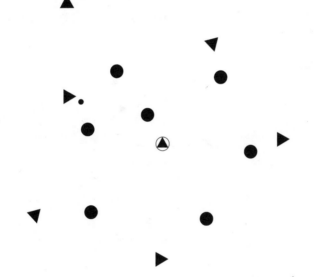

ORGANIZATION:	Game of 8 v 7 keep away.
INSTRUCTIONS:	One player (neutral player) plays on team in possession of ball.
COACHING POINTS:	• Use whole are in possession (spread defense). • Accurate passing. • Use numerical advantage to find open player. • Quick ball movement.
VARIATIONS:	Keep score by counting number of passes.

249

SMALL SIDED GAMES 109

OBJECTIVE:	Improving transition from offense to defense and vice versa
NUMBER OF PLAYERS:	15
AREA/FIELD:	Half field
TIME:	20-30 minutes
EQUIPMENT:	6 cones, supply of balls

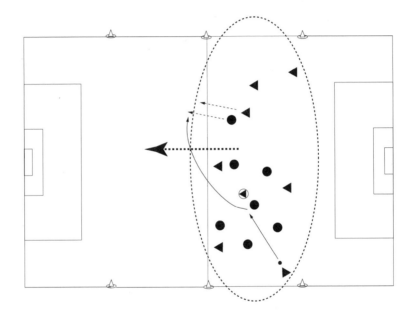

ORGANIZATION:	Game of 8 v 7 keep away on field divided in halves.
INSTRUCTIONS:	Team in possession plays keep away in own half. When defending team wins ball they switch quickly to their own half to play keep away. Both teams switch back and forth to halves when possession is won or lost. Neutral player plays on team in possession.

COACHING POINTS:
- Play "smart " possession.
- Use width and depth.
- Quick transition and switching halves.
- Look to play ball to own half as quick as possible when possession is won (look for long pass).

SMALL SIDED GAMES 110

OBJECTIVE:	Improving positional play in 8 v 8 game with 4 neutral players (numerical advantage)
NUMBER OF PLAYERS:	20
AREA/FIELD:	Half field
TIME:	20 minutes
EQUIPMENT:	16 cones, supply of balls

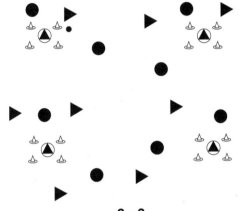

8 : 8
with 4 lay-off players

ORGANIZATION:	Two teams play 8 v 8 and can score by playing ball to neutral player.
INSTRUCTIONS:	• Neutral players can't leave grid. • To score, neutral player must receive pass and pass ball back to teammate.
COACHING POINTS:	• Create options and stretch defense by using whole playing area. • Look for neutral players quickly. • Movement to create options for neutral players. • Communication between team and neutral players.
VARIATIONS:	Each team has 2 set neutral players.

SMALL SIDED GAMES 111

OBJECTIVE: Creating game situations in small sided game

NUMBER OF PLAYERS: 21-24 plus 2 goalkeepers

AREA/FIELD: 50 yards x 35 yards

TIME: 20 minutes

EQUIPMENT: 4 cones, 2 goals, supply of balls

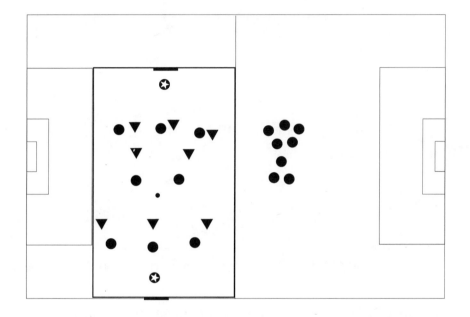

ORGANIZATION: 2 teams play 8 v 8 on 2 goals with 2 goalkeepers.

INSTRUCTIONS: Teams play until one team scores a goal. Team that scores stay on, team that loses switches positions with team waiting on side lines.

COACHING POINTS: • Try to score quickly without losing organization and shape.
• Play the correct rules (i.e. free-kicks, corner kicks, etc.)

253

SMALL SIDED GAMES 112

OBJECTIVE: Improving transition, linking up and communication

NUMBER OF PLAYERS: 16-20

AREA/FIELD: Three-fourths field

TIME: 30-40 minutes

EQUIPMENT: 4 cones, 2 goals, supply of balls

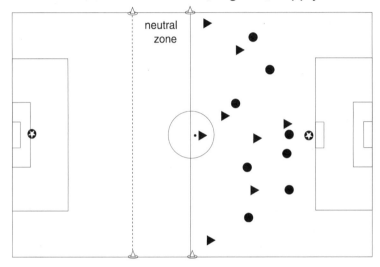

ORGANIZATION: Two teams play game on 3/4 field with 2 goalkeepers.

INSTRUCTIONS: Team in possession can only score when everybody is in their attacking zone. Dribbling in neutral zone is prohibited and can only be used for passing or combinations.

COACHING POINTS:
• Quick transition from defense to offense when ball is won back.
• Look to play ball deep to players in advanced positions quick transition from offense to defense; stop opposition from playing ball deep, pressure ball.

254

SMALL SIDED GAMES 113

OBJECTIVE:	Creating game situations in small sided game
NUMBER OF PLAYERS:	16 plus 2 goalkeepers
AREA/FIELD:	Two-thirds field
TIME:	20-30 minutes
EQUIPMENT:	6 cones, 2 goals, supply of balls

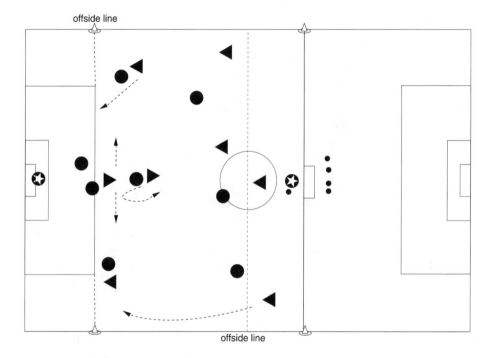

ORGANIZATION:	Two teams play 8 v 8 game on 2 goals with goalkeepers.
INSTRUCTIONS:	An offside line is put 18 yards out on each half of field.
COACHING POINTS:	Let players play in own positions and let them play with certain or specific objectives; overlaps, long ball to striker, etc.

SMALL SIDED GAMES 114

OBJECTIVE:	Improve diagonal passing and crosses and develop overlapping runs
NUMBER OF PLAYERS:	20
AREA/FIELD:	90 yards x 50 yards
TIME:	30 minutes
EQUIPMENT:	8 cones, 2 goals, supply of balls

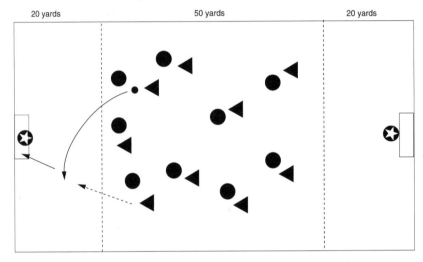

ORGANIZATION:	Two teams play 10v10 game on field 50 x 50 yards plus two 20 x 50 yard zones.
INSTRUCTIONS:	• Teams can only score from diagonal passes or cross passes into zone. • Pass must be in zone before player is.
COACHING POINTS:	• Time runs and passes to get scoring opportunities from cross passes. • Communication between passer and player receiving pass. • Create space to run and pass into. • Defenders and midfielders make overlapping runs.

SMALL SIDED GAMES 115

OBJECTIVE:	Improving 1 touch play
NUMBER OF PLAYERS:	14
AREA/FIELD:	20 yards x 30 yards
TIME:	10-15 minutes
EQUIPMENT:	4 cones, supply of balls

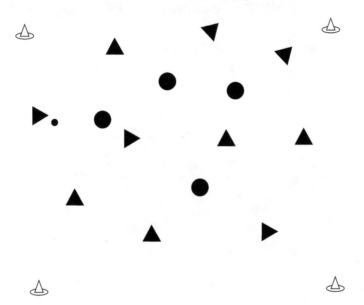

RONDO

ORGANIZATION:	Keep away game 10v4.
INSTRUCTIONS:	Defenders switch with attackers when they win possession.
COACHING POINTS:	• Everything 1 touch, be prepared and anticipate.
	• Create options for player in possession before he receives a pass.
	• Communication and eye contact.
VARIATIONS:	Keep defenders in middle for set time.

SMALL SIDED GAMES 116

OBJECTIVE:	Creating numerical advantage attacking from the back
NUMBER OF PLAYERS:	21
AREA/FIELD:	Two-thirds field
TIME:	20-30 minutes
EQUIPMENT:	8 cones, 2 goals, supply of balls

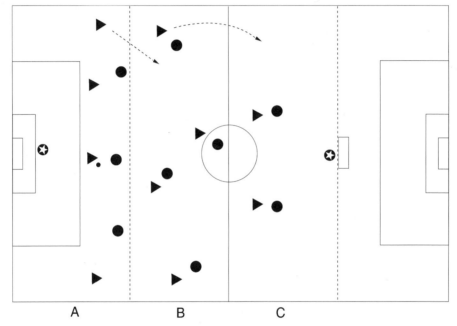

A   B   C

ORGANIZATION:
- Field is divided in 3 zones of 30 yards long.
- In zone A 4 players play 4v3 and attempt to pass ball to teammates in Zone B. In zone B a 5v4 will be created by 4 players in the zone plus one player from zone A. The same will be tried in zone C where a 3 v 2 will be created by 2 teammates plus a player from zone B. The 3 attackers in zone C attempt to score on goal.

258

SMALL SIDED GAMES 116

COACHING POINTS: • Use numerical advantage to keep possession, find open player and pass to teammate in next zone.
• Move ball around quickly but accurately.
• Play ball to next zone at right time.

VARIATIONS: Two players move up from zone B to zone A to create 4v2.

OBJECTIVE:	Improving positional play/keeping possession
NUMBER OF PLAYERS:	20
AREA/FIELD:	60 yards x 80 yards
TIME:	15-20 minutes
EQUIPMENT:	4 cones, supply of balls

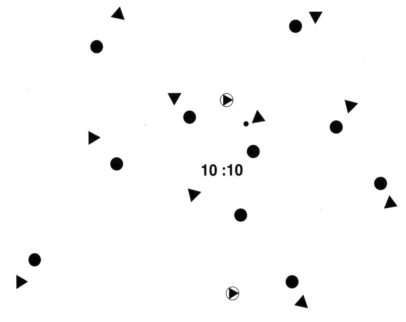

10 :10

ORGANIZATION:	10v10 keep away game.
INSTRUCTIONS:	Play 2 touch.
COACHING POINTS:	• All players in motion, always creating space, options and outlets. • Communication. • Keep team shape on offense and defense. • Quick ball circulation.
VARIATIONS:	Keep score by counting number of passes.